Toddler Hide and Seek

First words • Animals
Farm • Things that go

Notes for parents

Toddler Hide and Seek is a wonderful picture book for you and your child to share. From teddy bears, trains, and big-wheeled tractors to police cars, planets, and polar bears, it's filled with all sorts of interesting things to find and talk about. Every page provides lots of I-spy fun, and as children play, they build vocabulary, learn colours, practise counting, and develop observation skills.

To get the most out of this book

● Talk about all the things you can see on each page. Point to the objects, say their names, then hunt for each one together. As children become familiar with the book, they will be able to name and find the objects themselves.

● Encourage your child to describe the different things. What colour or shape are they? Do they have spots or stripes? What noises do they make? What are the vehicles used for? Which animal or object does your child like best?

● Read the rhymes and let your child say them with you. Then help your child find the objects in the rhymes.

● If your child knows letter sounds, you can play traditional I-spy. Ask your child to spot an object that begins with a certain letter.

Buzz!

DK Penguin Random House

Designed by
Rachael Parfitt Hunt
and Victoria Palastanga
Written by Dawn Sirett
Additional Text by Sarah Davis
Additional Editing by
Charlie Gardner and Phil Hunt
Illustrations by Angela Muss
and Paul Nicholls
Additional Illustrations by Rachael Parfitt
Hunt, Victoria Palastanga, and Dave Ball
Jacket Design Helen Senior
Special Additional Photography
Dave King
Design Assistance Nicola Price
Pre-Production Producers Andy Hilliard,
Siu Yin Chan, Jennifer Murray
Producers Louise Kelly, Jen Lockwood,
Danielle Smith, Andrew Beehag

2013 EDITION
Additional Pages Designed by
Alison Gardner
Additional Pages Edited by Dawn Sirett
Revised Index by Emma Callery
Special Sales Creative Project Manager
Alison Donovan
Pre-Production Producer
Rebecca Fallowfield
Producer Sarah Tanner

First published in Great Britain in 2013
This edition published in 2017
by Dorling Kindersley Limited
80 Strand, London WC2R 0RL

Material in this publication was
previously published in
Hide and Seek First Words (2010),
Hide and Seek Animals (2011),
Hide and Seek Farm (2012), and
Hide and Seek Things That Go (2013)

Copyright © 2010, 2011, 2012, 2013, 2017
Dorling Kindersley Limited
A Penguin Random House Company

3 5 7 9 10 8 6 5 4 2
002 – 197028 – Sept/13

A CIP catalogue record for this book
is available from the British Library.
ISBN 978-1-4093-3909-0

Printed and bound in China

A WORLD OF IDEAS:
SEE ALL THERE IS TO KNOW

www.dk.com

This is Buzzy Bee. He's hiding throughout this chapter. See if you can spot him in every scene!

first words

Toy shelf 6
Clothes 8
Animals 10
In the garden 12
Colours 14
Play school 16
Spots and stripes 18
At the beach 20
In the kitchen 22
Things that go 24
Play cooking 26
Busy builders 28
Black and white 30
Bathtime 32
Doll's house 34
On the farm 36
Musical things 38
Story time 40
Treasure hunt 42
Numbers 44
Christmas 46
More to find! 48

animals

Meow! 52
Woof! Woof! 54
My pets 56
On the farm 58
Creepy crawlies! 60
Tweet! 62
Wild woods 64
Reptiles 66
Splish! Splash! 68
Rivers 70
On safari 72
Jungle 74
Burrowers 76
Snowy animals 78
Baby animals 80
Dinosaurs 82
Matching 84
Animal patterns 86
Silhouettes 88
Counting 90
Look closer 92
More to find! 94

Ribbit!

This is Hoppity Frog! He's in every scene of this chapter. See if you can spot him again and again!

This is Dotty the Ladybird. She's hiding throughout this chapter. See if you can spot her in every scene!

Boo!

farm

Sheep and cows 98

Pigs and goats 100

Horses and donkeys 102

Farm birds 104

Animal groups 106

Tractors 108

More farm machines 110

Fruit and vegetables 112

Around the farm 114

Noisy farm 116

In the farm shed 118

Mummies and babies 120

At the farm shop 122

Farms around the world 124

Farm counting 126

Look closer 128

Farm silhouettes 130

What goes together? 132

Farm shapes 134

Farm colours 136

Toy farm 138

More to find! 140

things that go

On the road 144

Flying high! 146

Floating along 148

Trains and trams 150

Tough trucks 152

Roll, ride, slide! 154

At the building site 156

Emergency! 158

On the farm 160

At the races 162

Up in space! 164

Monster machines! 166

Parts and pieces 168

Motor maze! 170

Busy counting! 172

Wheels and tracks 174

Super silhouettes 176

What goes together? 178

Show me shapes! 180

Colour fun 182

Toy town 184

More to find! 186

This is Benjie Bus. He's in every scene of this chapter. See if you can spot him again and again!

Beep!

a dump truck

a pair of sparkly shoes

a spinning top

a rubber ring

a motorbike

Index of words we've found! 188

first words

This is Buzzy Bee.
He's hiding throughout this
chapter. See if you can spot him
in every scene!

Toy shelf

Let's find...

a duck

a teddy

a ball

a train

a doll

a tower of stacking cups

a camera

a spinning top

a jar of marbles

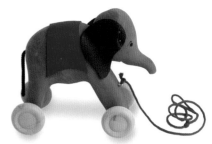
a penguin

an elephant

a caterpillar

a snail

a drum

a crocodile

a cat

a rocket

3 wooden people

2 fire engines

a firefighter

a robot

a dinosaur

a hobby horse

I spy a racing car.
If you see it, you're a star!

7

Clothes
Let's find...

some
pyjamas

a vest

a pair
of pants

a dressing
gown

a pair
of slippers

2 jumpers

a pair
of trainers

a pair of
dungarees

a watch

a dress

a skirt

a jacket

a scarf

a pair
of socks

a pair of
sparkly shoes

a pair of
trousers

a hairbrush

a comb

2 white
buttons

a belt

a raincoat

an umbrella

8

Choose your
favourite thing to wear,
then find a little
teddy bear.

Animals
Let's find...

a spider

an elephant

a giraffe

a horse

a mouse

a dinosaur

a kangaroo and joey

a dog

a lion

a hippo

2 snakes

3 ducks

a zebra

a pig

a crocodile

a cow

a frog

a rabbit

10

Which creature
has been caught
for lunch?
Can he escape
before he's
munched?

11

In the garden

Let's find...

a butterfly

4 bulbs

a trowel

a spider

3 snails

a stripy
plant pot

a yellow
watering can

a ball
of string

a dragonfly

3 ladybirds

a frog

a fork

a pair
of gloves

2 sunflowers

a bird

a bird house

a rake

a pair
of wellies

Can you see a tiny man with his own small watering can?

Seeds

13

Colours

Let's find...

a green paintbrush

a red lipstick

a purple comb

a man in blue

a yellow bus

a green bug

an orange flower

a red mouse

a green leaf

a purple butterfly

14

a yellow chick

 an orange bracelet

 1 green circle

 3 orange triangles

 2 blue rectangles

 a blue dinosaur

 a red strawberry

 3 yellow squares

 7 purple stars

 1 red heart

If you can find a tiny bed, you'll spot a teeny sleepyhead!

Play school

Let's find...

a painting

a pair of scissors

a pencil case

a frog calculator

a skipping rope

a ruler

3 crayons

a pencil sharpener

a stapler

a football rubber

3 tubes of glitter

a blackboard

a pair of glasses

a pen

a paint palette

3 paintbrushes

a piece of chalk

a magnet

3 red stars

a glue pen

a magnifying glass

a clock

4 bottles of paint

2 toy children

a notebook

a globe

I spy a little cat somewhere. It was made at school with great care.

Spots and stripes

Let's find...

a present

a doggy rattle

5 red-and-white toadstools

a caterpillar

a leopard

a domino

a fish

a red-and-wh
bow

18

a rainbow
purse

a notebook

4 pencils

a pair
of mittens

a rainbow

a tiger

a plate

a cup
and saucer

a woolly hat

a dice

a teddy

Meow! Meow!
Who said that?
Where's the stripy
knitted cat?

At the beach
Let's find...

a sandcastle

2 sailing boats

a kite

a pair of sandals

a cap

a pair of binoculars

a swimming costume

a bucket

a dolphin

a spade

a flag

a pair of swimming trunks

4 pebbles

a pair of sunglasses

a pair of flippers

a rubber ring

a snorkel

an ice-cream

a mask

a windmill

Somewhere
at the beach I spy
a scaly turtle creeping by.

In the kitchen

Let's find...

a mug

a colander

a grater

a kettle

a vase of flowers

3 spoons

a clock

a box of tissues

a bowl of fruit

a framed photo

a blue jug

a spatula

a tea towel

a pair of tongs

3 bowls

a vegetable peeler

a casserole dish

a washing-up brush

3 hooks

a blue serving spoon

a sieve

2 keys

a tray

a saucepan

I spy two big eyes and a mouth so wide
you can fit a kitchen sponge inside!

Things that go

Let's find...

a motorbike

2 blue-and-red planes

a hot-air balloon

a sailing boat

2 orange-and-green racing cars

3 red cars

a jeep

a scooter

a tractor with loader

a helicopter

a truck

a rubbish truck

a bus

a fire engine

24

Look at all
the things to drive,
then find the number 55.

Play cooking
Let's find...

a jar
of jam

a blue
mixing bowl

3 biscuits

a rolling pin

a heart
pastry cutter

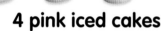

4 pink iced cakes

a jelly
mould

4 pasta shapes

an oven
glove

a spoon

a knife

a fork

4 empty cake cases

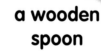

a wooden
spoon

some raisins

a whisk

a weighing
scale

a cake stand

Spot three candles on three cakes, and two hearts cut out to bake.

Busy builders

Let's find...

7 stripy cones

a tipper truck

a wheel loader

a backhoe loader

2 drills

a bulldozer

One busy builder
has a call from home.
Can you see the
mobile phone?

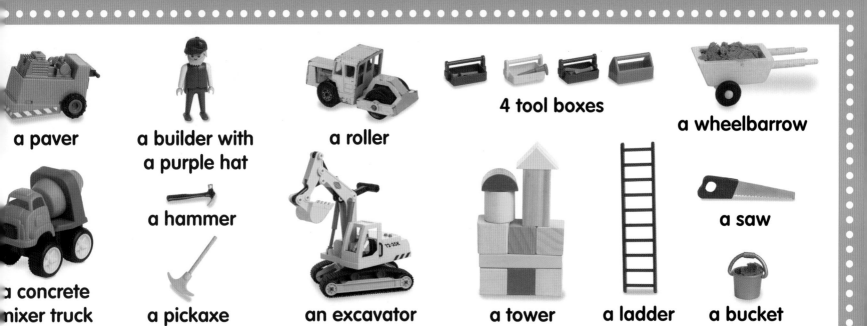

a paver

a builder with
a purple hat

a roller

4 tool boxes

a wheelbarrow

a concrete
mixer truck

a hammer

a pickaxe

an excavator

a tower

a ladder

a saw

a bucket

Black and white

Let's find...

a magician's wand

a bow tie

a rabbit

a pair of
glasses

2 wheels

a polar bear

a pair of shoes

a piano

2 ghosts

a panda

Find a mouse
playing
a tune,
and a couple
marrying soon!

skeleton

a blackbird

an egg

3 bats

a plastic hat

cauldron

8 dominoes

a monkey

3 footballs

3 black cats

a Dalmatian

Bathtime
Let's find...

 a fishing net

 a butterfly soap

 a bottle of shampoo

 a yellow towel

 a crab

 a soap dish

 a bottle of bubble bath

 a mermaid

 a nailbrush

 a starfish

 a seal

 a seahorse

 3 toothbrushes

 a big yellow duck

 a blue-and-yellow diver

 2 green boats

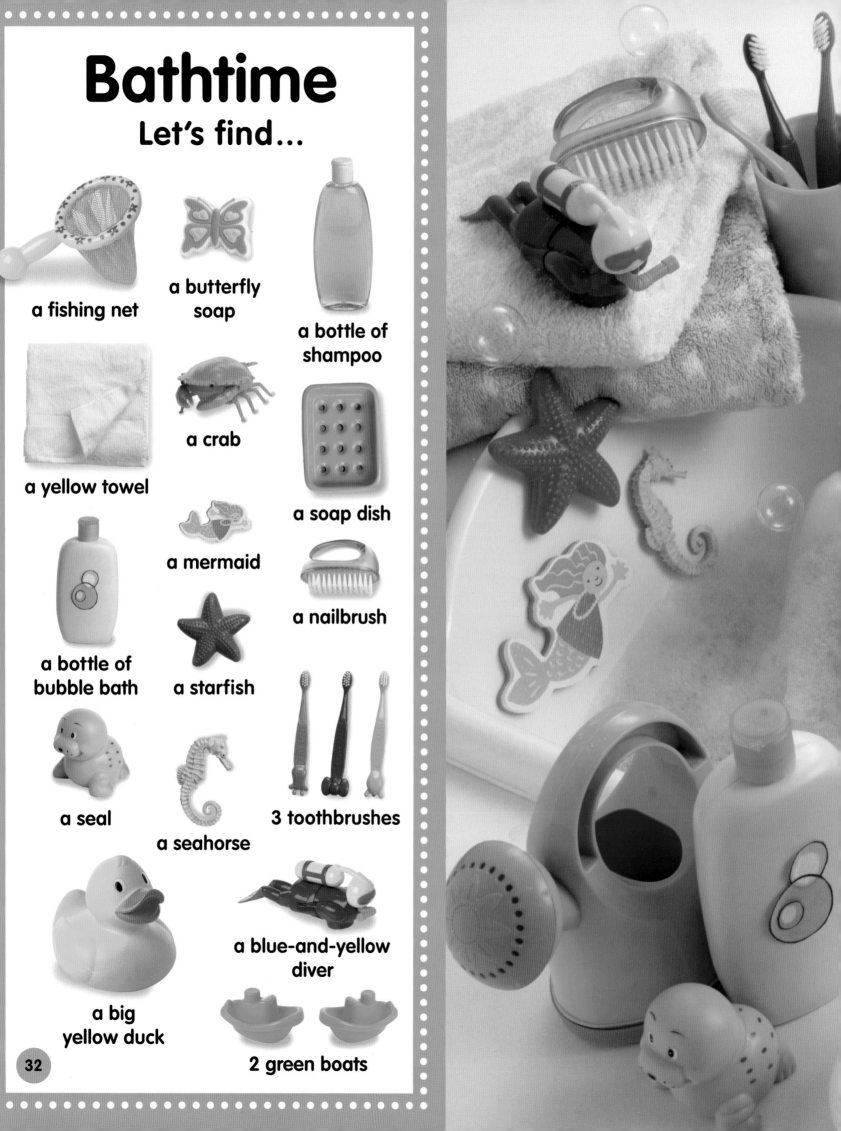

Look here, there... ...and everywhere for six bubbles in the air.

33

Doll's house

Let's find...

a bath

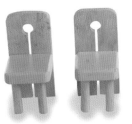
2 pink chairs

a bike

a lamp

a toaster

a bunk bed

a rabbit hutch

a green chest of drawers

a sofa

a shower

a table

Dad, Mum, 2 children, and the baby

a kitchen sink

a highchair

a saucepan

a train

a cooker

a pram

a rocking horse

a bed

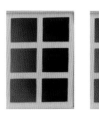
a toilet

2 big windows

a cot

a highchair

a television

a computer

a cooker

I spy with my little eye
a dog and a rabbit, and a cat up high.

35

On the farm

Let's find...

 a tractor

 4 ducklings

a donkey

2 farmers

 2 cows

2 sheep

4 hens

a cockerel

36

4 horses

2 milk churns

a basket of vegetables

a dog

a kennel

a tyre

turkey

a kid

a goat

a pitchfork

a pig

2 piglets

a pigsty

a green ladder

Somewhere hiding
for you to seek,
are three farm mice.
Squeak, squeak, squeak!

37

Musical things
Let's find...

a recorder

a trumpet

2 cymbals

a xylophone

2 shakers

a triangle

8 gold bells

a drum

2 harmonicas

a bongo drum

an accordion

a tambourine

3 kazoos

an electric guitar

a keyboard

Spy a frog that goes click click. You can do it – you're so quick!

39

Story time

Let's find...

the Queen

the King

a dragon

a witch's cat

a glass slipper

2 ballerinas

a horse and carriage

a tow

a witch

2 princesses

a fairy godmother

the moon

2 fairies

3 fish

a lion

a prince

a mermaid

a superhero

a wizard

Spot two magic wands, then here's what you do...

...make a special wish that you'd like to come true!

Treasure hunt

Let's find...

a treasure chest

a key

a parrot

a crown

a pirate ship

a gold buckle

a green heart jewel

6 wooden pirates

a charm bracelet

a monkey

10 gold coins

a brooch

a fob watch

a treasure map

a sword

a book

a compass

a quill pen

a starfish

a telescope

a ruby ring

a scroll

a pirate's hat

More sparkly jewels are buried in the ground. I spy the "X" where they can be found!

Numbers

Let's find the number...

 zero

 one

 two

 three

 four

 five

 six

 seven

 eight

 nine

 ten

 eleven

 twelve

 thirteen

 fourteen

 fifteen

 sixteen

 seventeen

 eighteen

 nineteen

twenty

fifty

 one hundred

Now let's count...

 2 rainbows

2 green stars

3 yellow planets

 5 candles

How old are you? Please tell me.
And where's that number? Can you see?

Christmas
Let's find...

a penguin

a Christmas tree

a tiny Santa

an owl

a red spotty bauble

a dancing Santa

2 candy canes

a teddy

a sledge and rider

a spotty star

an angel

2 snowmen

3 blue sweets

2 pinecones

a reindeer

a stocking

5 green baubles

To Santa
North Pole

Find a letter. Who's it to? What would you write if it was from you?

47

More to find!

You'll find all these things if you go back and look in the first busy chapter of this hide-and-seek book!

 a lemon

 a mirror

 a red spotty kettle

 a police car

 a saxophone

 3 skateboards

 a yellow spatula

a cake slice

 an orange cat clock

a bookshelf

 a yellow concrete mixer

 a car transporter

 2 cowboys

 2 oranges

a slice of orange

 a pair of tights

 a green tractor

 a tomato

 a bag of flour

 a pirate skull eyepatch

"Bye-bye!" says Buzzy Bee. "How many times did you spot me?"

Bye-bye!

4 blue
potty clouds

a coat stand

a deckchair

a broom

a red
cotton reel

silver whistle

3 suns

a bird and
birdcage

an apple tree

7 more trees

a torch

a little
chef

a yellow sponge

a packet
of seeds

an armchair

2 red sweets

a rose ring

an abacus

a dog bowl

a bale
of wheat

animals

Ribbit!

This is Hoppity Frog!
He's in every scene of this
chapter. See if you can spot
him again and again!

Meow!

Let's find...

5 Siamese cats

a cat collar

a silver
spotted cat

4 cat paw prints

a Manx cat
(a cat with no tail)

a brown cat

a toy cat

a black cat

a red tabby cat

a cream cat and
a grey kitten

a black-and-white
cat

a Sphynx cat

3 toy mice

a silver-blue cat

I spy a cat
in front of the moon.
I think
you'll spot him
very soon.

a Birman cat

a Persian cat

a tortoiseshell cat

Woof! Woof!

Let's find...

a German Shepherd

a Beagle

a Pomeranian

a Miniature Schnauzer

a Pug

a Poodle

a Cocker Spaniel

54

3 Dachshunds

2 Labradors

Find the doggy bones.
There are three.
Where are they hiding?
Can you see?

**a Bulldog
and 2 puppies**

a dog lead

4 food bowls

2 Shih tzu

2 Chihuahuas

a toy dog

My pets

Let's find...

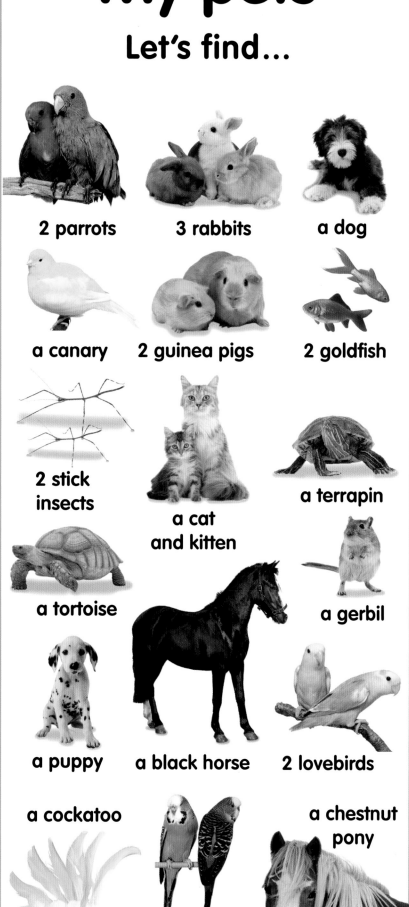

2 parrots

3 rabbits

a dog

a canary

2 guinea pigs

2 goldfish

2 stick insects

a cat and kitten

a terrapin

a tortoise

a gerbil

a puppy

a black horse

2 lovebirds

a cockatoo

2 budgies

a chestnut pony

Mirror, mirror
on the wall,
where's the reptile
with no legs
at all?

57

On the farm

Let's find...

a black sheep

2 geese

a black-and-white cow

4 white ducks

a spotty p

a cockere

58

a calf

4 lambs

3 piglets

billy goat

a sheep dog

a foal

a donkey

a black-and-white bull

I spy a mouse upon the ground. When you see him, make a squeaky sound!

59

Creepy crawlies!

Let's find...

3 spiders

4 flies

a millipede

a wasp

4 snails

a dragonfly

2 crickets

2 bees

3 butterflies

a beetle

a locust

a moth

5 slugs

a thorn bug

2 earthworms

6 fireflies

7 ladybirds

a mite

2 leaf insects

6 woodlice

2 caterpillars

a digger wasp

a spider
hunting wasp

4 stag
beetles

Can you find five marching ants? I hope they're not inside your pants!

Tweet!
Let's find...

2 macaws

a puffin

a vulture

a woodpecker

a blackbird

a mallard

a rainbow lorikeet

a hummingbird

2 magpies

a swallow

a spoonbill

a dove

an ostrich

3 swans

a kingfisher

Spot the eggs
laid in a nest,
then choose the bird
that you like best.

63

Wild Woods

Let's find...

2 bald eagles

a grey squirrel

a grizzly bear

2 foxes

a white-tailed deer

a white-tailed fawn

an American beaver

a raco

64

a striped
skunk

an American
porcupine

a weasel

I see an owl.
Can you see him, too?
When you do,
shout, "Twit-twoo!"

goshawk

a black bear

a rat snake

6 wild rabbits

3 cardinal
birds

a wild boar

Reptiles

Let's find...

2 tortoises

a crocodile

a caiman

a Thai water dragon

a glass lizard

a chameleon

a western diamondback rattlesnake

a spotty, stripy gecko

a Gila monster

a milk snake

a rat snake

a European green lizard

a desert iguana

an alligator

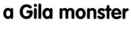

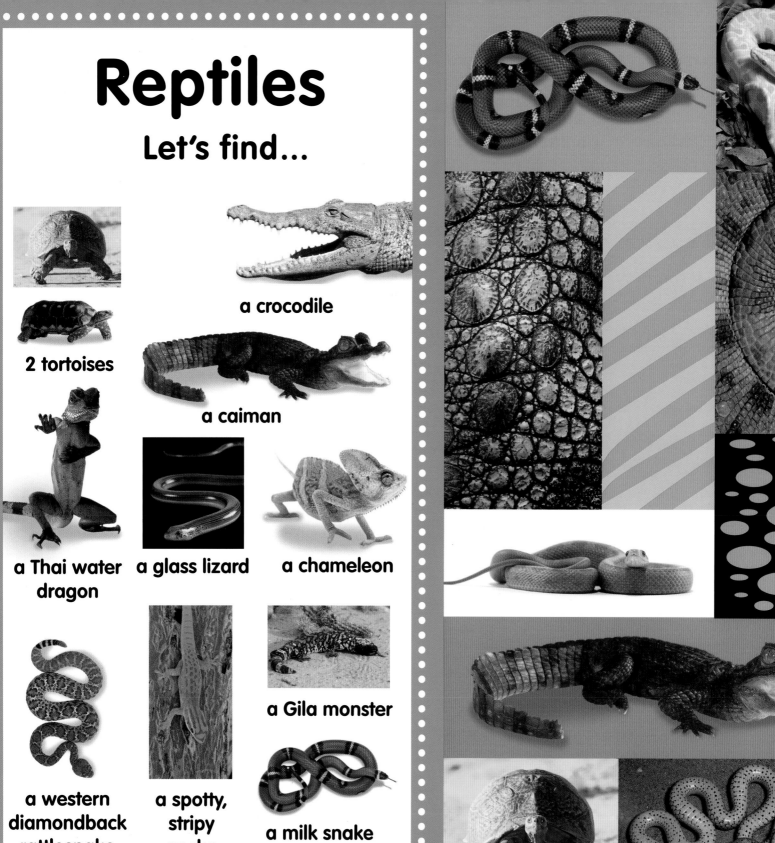

Floating
oh so gracefully,
find two turtles
in the sea.

Splish! Splash!

Let's find...

3 hermit crabs

3 seahorses

2 green sea turtles

5 brown starfish

a killer whale

2 banded sea snake

an oc sunfi

68

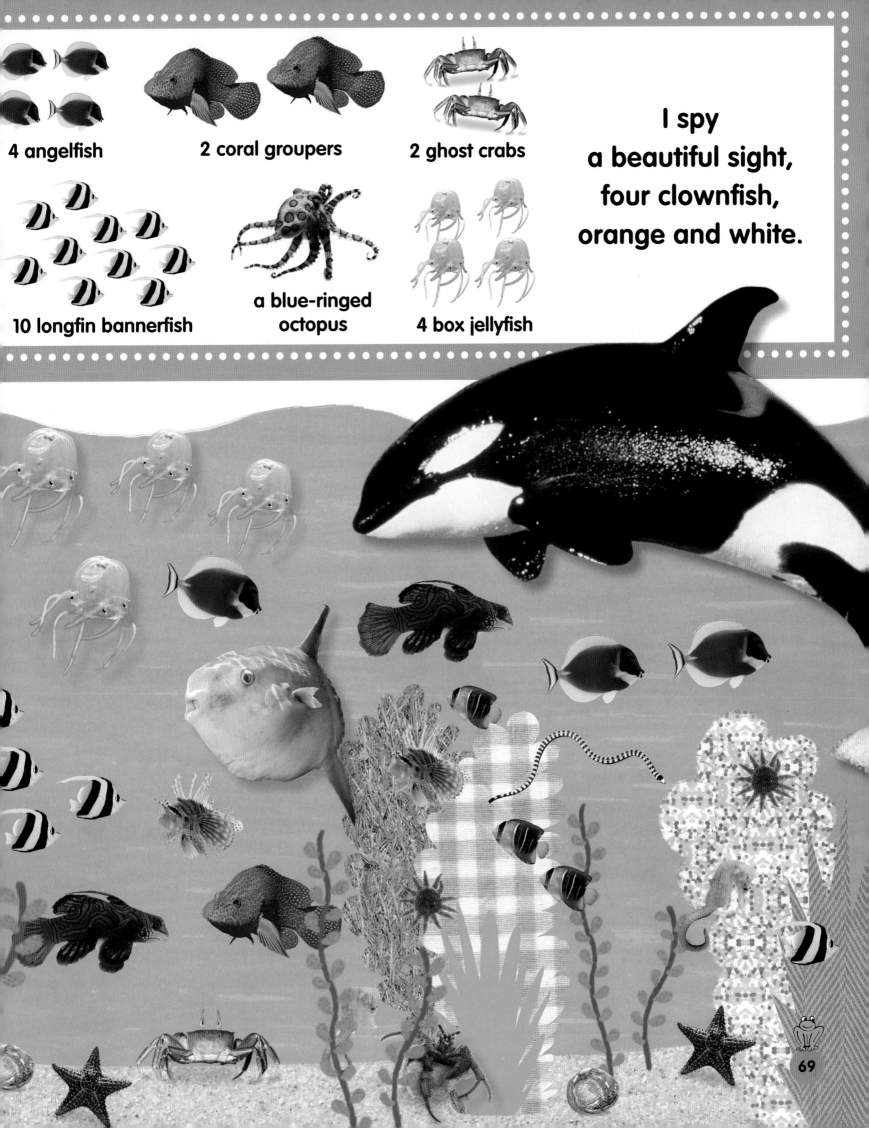

4 angelfish

2 coral groupers

2 ghost crabs

10 longfin bannerfish

a blue-ringed octopus

4 box jellyfish

I spy
a beautiful sight,
four clownfish,
orange and white.

69

Rivers
Let's find...

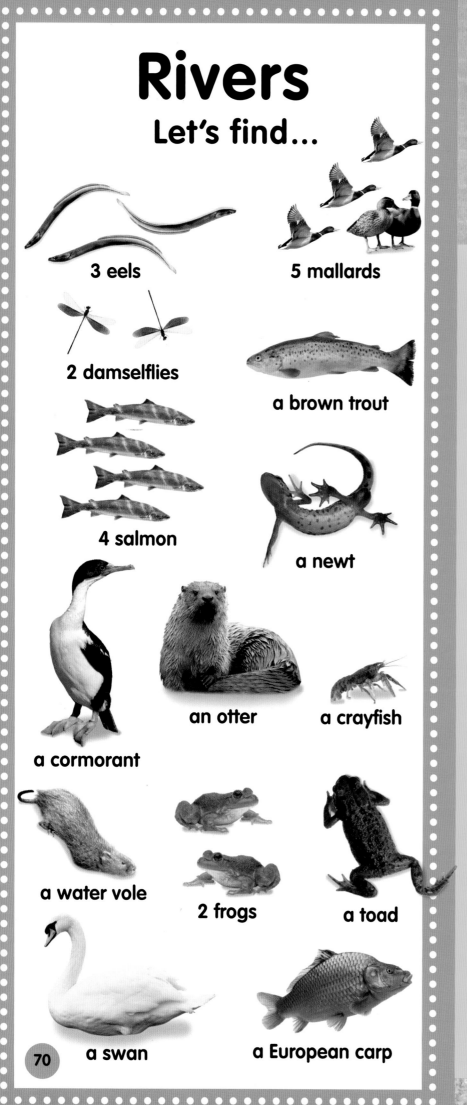

3 eels

5 mallards

2 damselflies

a brown trout

4 salmon

a newt

a cormorant

an otter

a crayfish

a water vole

2 frogs

a toad

a swan

a European carp

Look for three small blue-eyed fish called sticklebacks, splish, splash, splish!

On safari

Let's find...

3 giraffes

an African elephant

6 harvester ants

2 zebras

an African bison

a bushbaby

72

a white
rhinoceros

a warthog

2 secretary
birds

a lion and lioness

a gazelle

a baboon

a cheetah

a bat-eared
fox

a jackal

I spy
two
porcupines.
Watch out
for their
prickly spines!

73

Jungle

Let's find...

a chimpanzee

4 morpho butterflies

a toucan

a jaguar

a poison dart frog

an orang-utan

5 piranhas

a gorilla

a red-eyed tree frog

a tarantula

an Asian elephant

a chameleon

a jumping spider

a sloth

a tiger

Five stripy beetles, can you find them all?
Look carefully, for they are quite small.

Burrowers

Let's find...

a fox

a pocket mouse

a mole

7 ants

an American badger

a prairie dog

a thirteen-lined ground squirrel

a chipmun

a hooded skunk

a black-footed ferret

a burrowing owl

groundhog

a bull snake

a six-lined race runner

4 rabbits

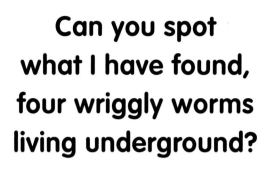

Can you spot what I have found, four wriggly worms living underground?

77

Snowy animals
Let's find...

an emperor
penguin

a walrus

a Greenland shark

a great
grey owl

an ermine

2 Arctic foxes

a polar
bear cub

an icefish

a beluga
whale

a wolverine

a bearded seal

a crab-eater
seal

a grey seal
pup

a snowy owl

a lemming

a narwhal

a reindeer

a grey wolf

Where's the
Arctic hare?
I think I know.
Her winter fur
is as white as snow.

79

Baby animals

Let's find...

an ostrich chick

a Dachshund
puppy

4 penguin chicks

5 ducklings

a fawn

an elephant calf

6 baby rabbits

a lion cub

2 fox cubs

a seal pup

a lamb

4 kittens

2 owl chicks

a pony foal

3 piglets

**Are you clever?
Are you quick?
Can you spot
a yellow chick?**

Dinosaurs

Let's find...

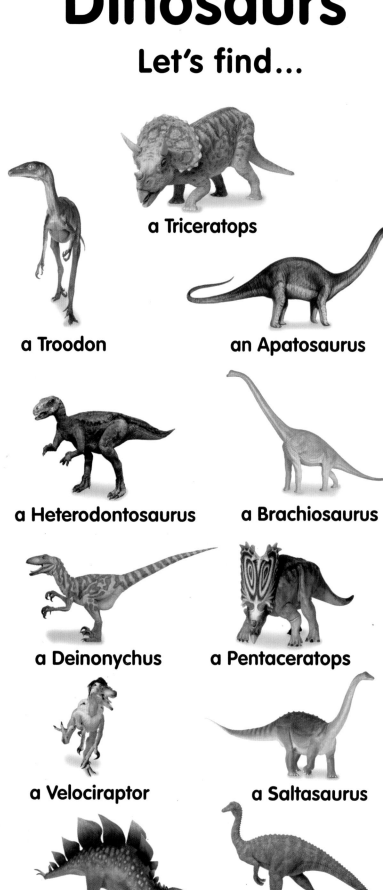

a Triceratops

a Troodon

an Apatosaurus

a Heterodontosaurus

a Brachiosaurus

a Deinonychus

a Pentaceratops

a Velociraptor

a Saltasaurus

a Stegosaurus

a Gallimimus

I spy a
frightening sight,
a mighty T-rex
about to bite!

Matching

Let's find the other halves of these jigsaw animals.

a seal

a jay

a ring-tailed lemur

a Chinese peacock butterfly

a dolphin

There are five caterpillars for you to seek.
Count them as they crawl and creep.

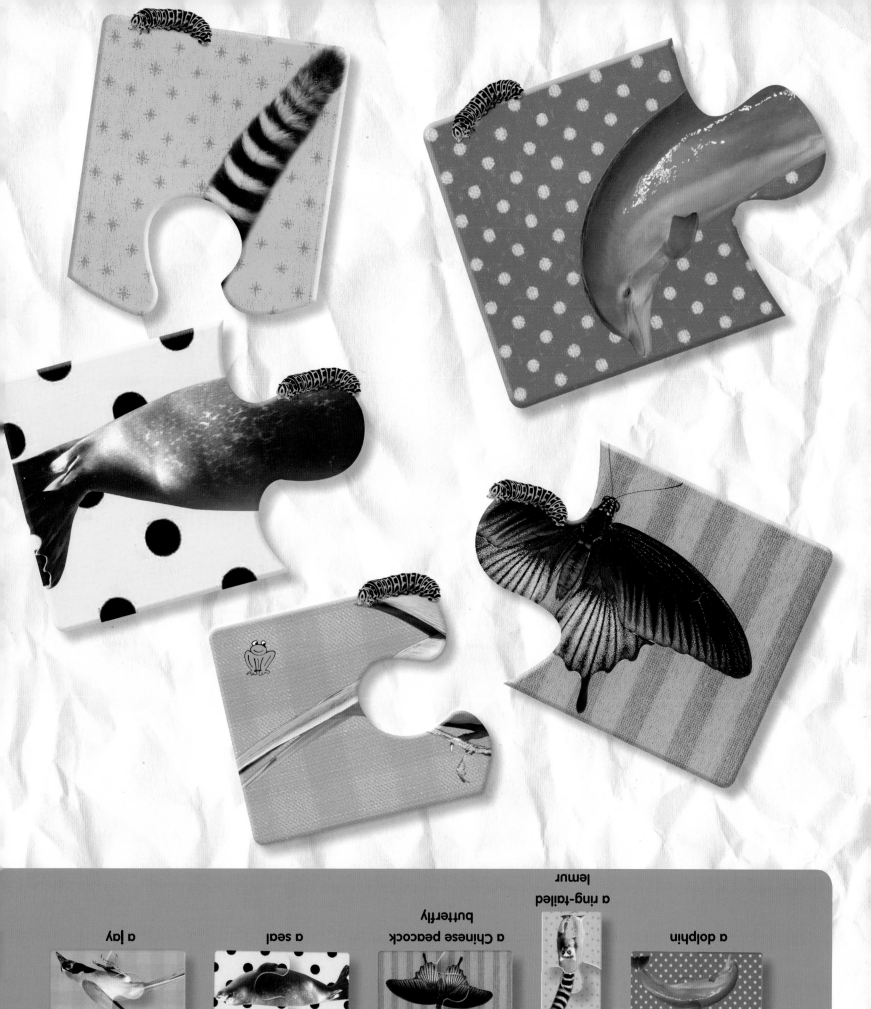

Animal patterns

Let's find the pattern for...

a tiger

a killer whale

an elephant

a toucan

a zebra

a chick

an elephant

a cheetah

a butterfly

a frog

a flamingo

a koala

a beetle

a kitten

a ladybird

a snake

There are six stripy moths
I can see.
Where have they landed?
Please show me.

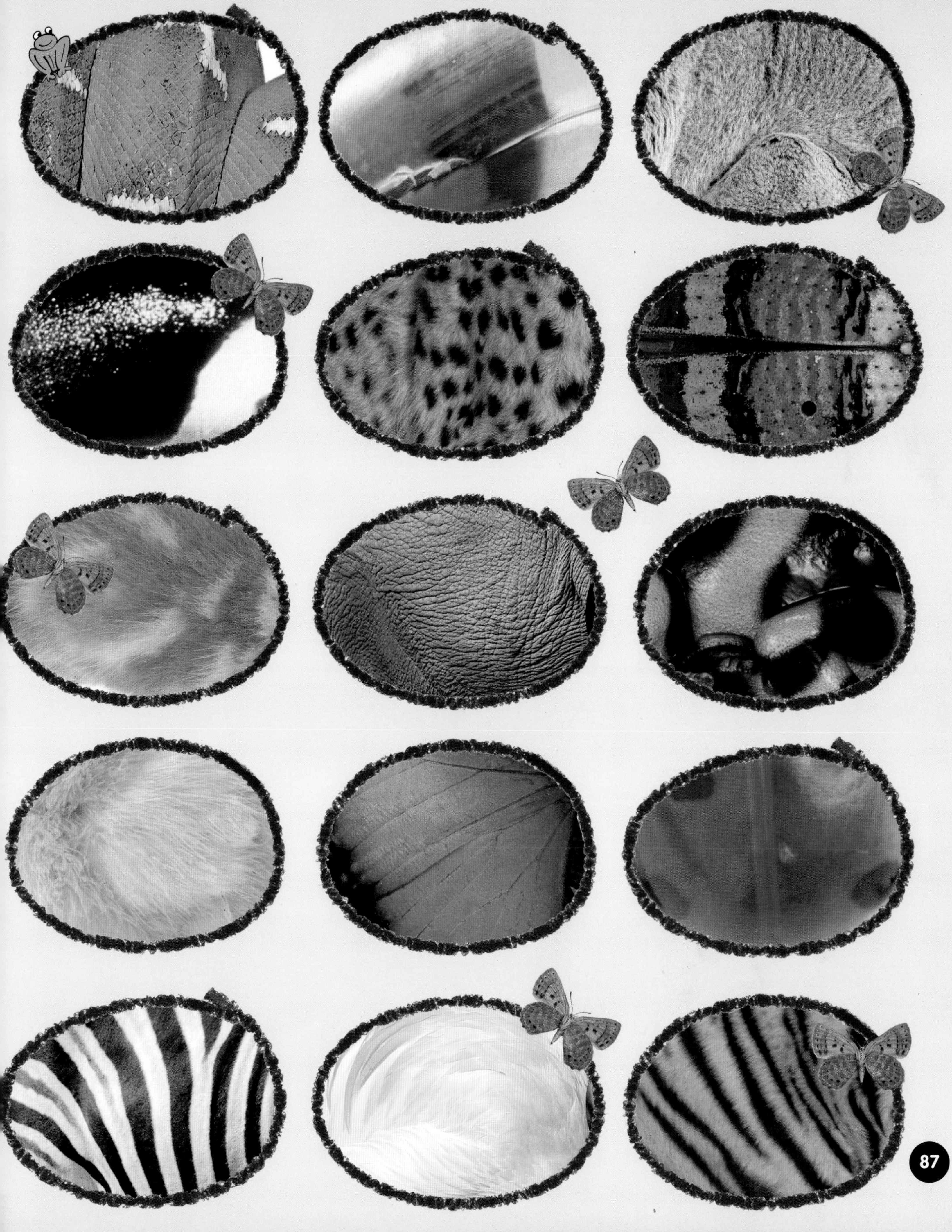

Silhouettes

Let's find...

a sea lion

a kangaroo

2 houseflies

an ostrich

3 centipedes

an aardvark

a bat

a puffin

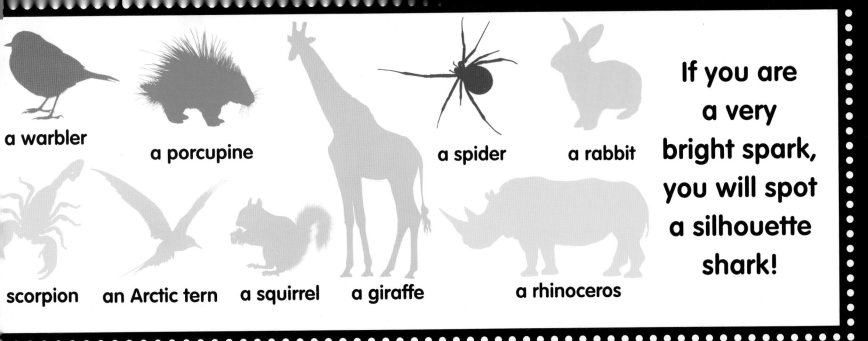

a warbler

a porcupine

a spider

a rabbit

scorpion

an Arctic tern

a squirrel

a giraffe

a rhinoceros

If you are a very bright spark, you will spot a silhouette shark!

Counting

Let's find...

1 panda

2 chimpanzees

Count twenty snails
one by one,
for counting creatures
is such fun!

3 butterflies

4 armadillos

5 rabbits

6 cats

7 dogs

8 insects

9 birds

10 fish

Look closer

Let's find a close-up of...

a cat

a coral grouper

a tree frog

a reindeer

a seahorse

a tiger

a pig

a snail

a beetle

a clownfish

a dog

a goldfish

a Stegosaurus

a zebra

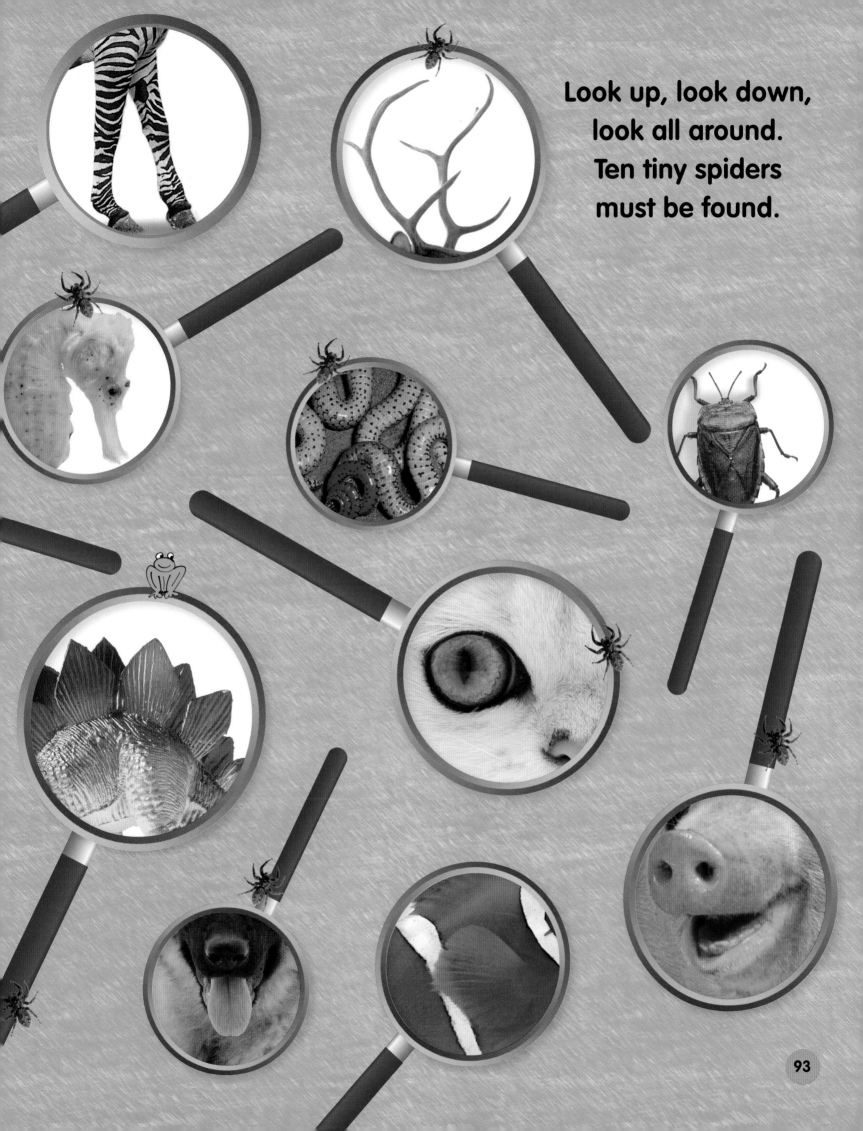

Look up, look down,
look all around.
Ten tiny spiders
must be found.

93

More to find!

You'll find all these things if you go back and look in the Animals chapter of this hide-and-seek book!

2 snake silhouettes

a cat basket

a brown tabby cat

a blue dog kennel with a red roof

2 dog balls

3 toadstools

8 blue paw prints

2 buckets

a Diplodocus

a volcano

a horseshoe

2 Golden Retriever puppies

2 guinea fowl

13 clouds

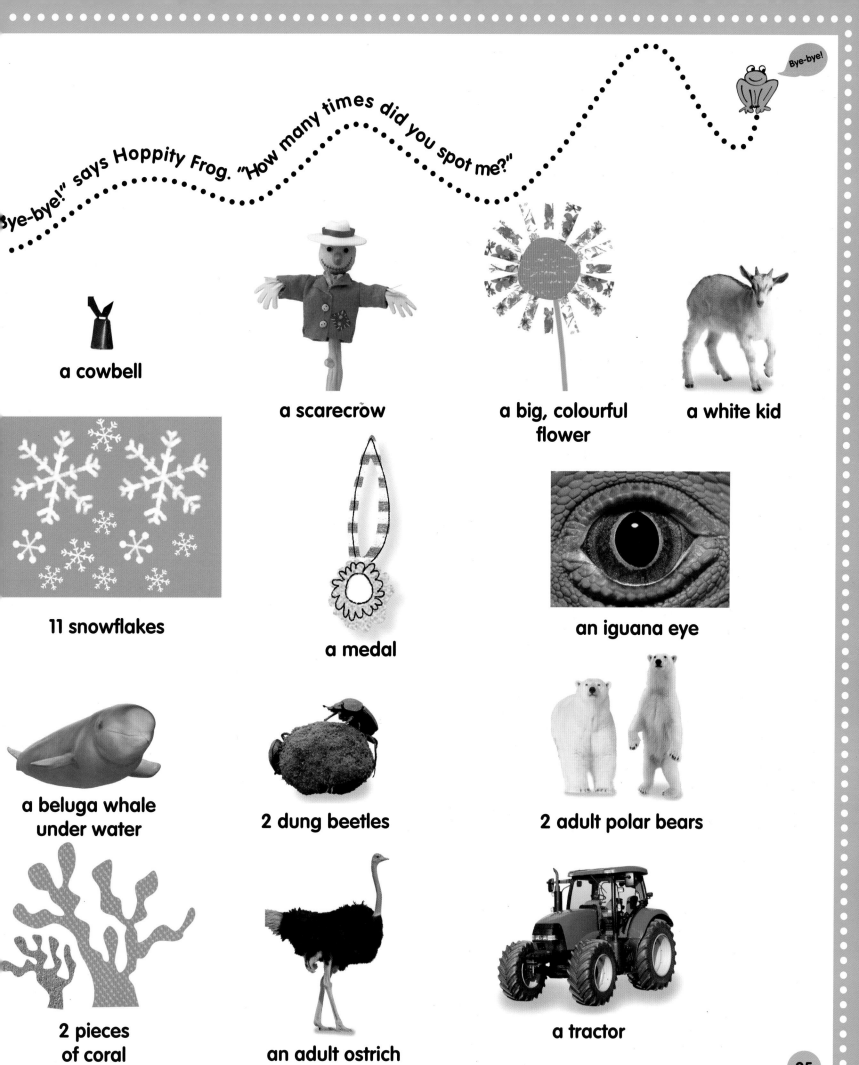

"Bye-bye!" says Hoppity Frog. "How many times did you spot me?"

a cowbell

a scarecrow

a big, colourful flower

a white kid

11 snowflakes

a medal

an iguana eye

a beluga whale under water

2 dung beetles

2 adult polar bears

2 pieces of coral

an adult ostrich

a tractor

farm

Boo!

This is Dotty the Ladybird. She's hiding throughout this chapter. See if you can spot her in every scene!

Sheep and cows

Let's find...

a ewe with 2 lambs

5 black-faced sheep

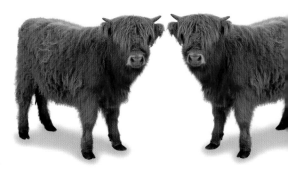

2 hairy brown cows

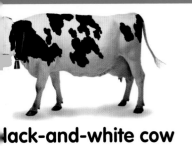

black-and-white cow

2 short-haired brown cows

2 brown-and-white calves a ram

ink daisies

3 black-and-white calves

2 milk churns

Baa! Baa!
Moo! Moo!
Spot a black bull
and a black sheep, too.

99

Pigs and goats

Let's find...

3 buckets

2 kids

a brown nanny goat

a carton of goat's milk

some goat's cheese

a black pig with a pink stripe

a curly-haired billy goat

a sow with 6 piglets

a spotty pig

a boar

a pig in a pigsty

I see a pig's trough
and a shiny goat's bell.
If you can spot them,
you're doing very well.

Horses and donkeys

Let's find...

a horse and cart

a grey horse

6 horseshoes

a donkey carrying a pack

a saddle

2 white shire horses

a chestnut horse

a mare with her foal

a riding hat

a horse and rider

a white horse

a donkey with her foal

a black stallion

a medal

a white horse with brown spots

Best Horse

Find two rosettes,
and read
what they say.
Then choose
who should wear
each rosette today.

Best
Donkey

Farm birds
Let's find...

5 yellow chicks

a pheasant

a cockerel

a white Aylesbury duck

a duck house

3 Indian Runner ducks

3 geese and 2 goslings

a chick that has just hatched

4 yellow ducklings

a turkey

4 yellow feathers

a brown hen

a guinea fowl

Can you find nine eggs?
I will count them all with you.
Three of them are hatching.
We need to count those, too.

Animal groups

Let's find...

a herd of pigs

a litter of baby rabbits

a herd of cows

a flock of mallard ducks

a herd of deer

a litter of
sheepdog puppies

a herd of goats

a litter of piglets

a flock of sheep

a brood
of ducklings

a gaggle of geese

a clutch
of chicks

A team of five horses
are pulling a plough.
When you can see them,
shout, "Giddy-up now!"

Tractors

Let's find...

a blue
cabless tractor

a green tractor pulling a blue tra

a red tractor pulling a plough

3 stacked tyres

a green eight-wheeled tract

5 toy tractors

a red tractor with a loader

a pink tractor

an orange tractor pulling a manure spreader

an old red tractor

Point to the tractor that's lifting a bale of hay. Then choose one busy tractor you'd like to drive today.

More farm machines

Let's find...

a trailer carrying hay bales

an all-terrain vehicle

a pick-up truck

a loader with a grapple fork

a combine harvester

a crop-spraying plane

a skid-steer loader

an off-road vehicle

a logging truck

a horsebox

a rice harvester

a grape harvester

a baler

Where is the milk tanker?
Do you know?
With milk from the dairy,
it's ready to go!

Fruit and vegetables

Let's find...

3 slices of cucumber

a box of oranges

2 corn on the cobs

7 apples

a slice of **watermelon**

6 mushrooms

a pumpk

4 strawberries

carrots

an onion

a tray of courgettes

lettuce

a sack of potatoes

a bunch of bananas

5 tomatoes

I spy some fruit
for our lunch,
red cherries
in a basket
and green grapes
in a bunch.

113

Around the farm
Let's find...

3 mice

a scarecrow

2 doves

a snail

a squirrel

a frog

2 ducks

a beehive

a sheepdog

a black cat

an owl

2 rabbits

3 sunflowers

3 cygnets

a fence

Where are
the foxes?
Can you see?
Count them with me.
There are three.

Noisy farm

Let's find the noise each animal makes, then say the funny noises together.

a cockerel
goes…

a mouse
goes…

a chick
goes…

a frog
goes…

a goose
goes…

a sheepdog
goes…

a kitten
goes…

an owl
goes…

a duck
goes…

a cow goes…

a pig goes…

a lamb goes…

a goat goes…

a donkey
goes…

a horse
goes…

I spy
twelve busy buzzy bees.
Can you help me count them please?

mooo!

twit-twoo!

baaaa!

quack! quack!

squeak! squeak!

neigh!

meow!

honk! honk!

oink! oink!

cheep! eep!

cooo! cooo!

ribbit! ribbit!

naaa!

woof! woof!

eee-aw!

cock-a-doodle-doo!

117

In the farm shed

Let's find...

a sack

2 cats and
3 kittens

a pair of goggles

2 pairs of gloves

a crate of herbs

a basket of logs

a bucket

a rope

a pair of
ear protectors

a tool box

a saw

a spanner

a fork

a shovel

a spade

an axe

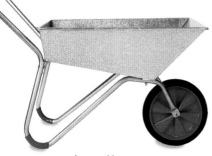
a wheelbarrow

a rake

I see three pairs of wellies.
Can you find them all?
Two pairs are big,
and the third is very small.

a broom

Mummies and babies

Let's find the baby that belongs to each mummy animal.

a sheep

a pig

a goat

a chicken

an owl

a rabbit

a sheepdog

a cat

a donkey

a fox

a goose

a cow

a horse

There are seven
yellow ducklings
waddling around.
When you've
found them all,
make a noisy
quack, quack sound!

121

At the farm shop

Let's find...

a string of garlic

2 bunches of herbs

an apple tart

2 big bottles
of milk

a block of butter

2 bags of flour

a wedge
of cheese

a loaf of bread

2 jars of strawberry jam

a tub of muesli

3 pots
of yoghurt

some strings
of sausages

3 bottles of
apple juice

6 eggs in a carton

a jar
of biscuits

I spy something sweet and runny,
a jar of golden, sticky honey.

Farms around the world

Let's find...

a flower farm

a tea plantation

a salmon farm

a sugar cane plantation

a coconut plantation

an apple orchard

a rice farm

a cattle ranch

a cotton plantation

a bee farm

a banana plantation

a chilli pepper farm

a vineyard

a coffee plantation

What more can we find
on our I-spy trail?
Three horses
on a stud farm.
That's where horses
are for sale.

a bison ranch

125

Farm Counting

Let's find...

1 horse

2 flowers

3 piglets

4 lambs

5 chickens

6 chilli peppers

7 goats

8 lettuces

9 cows

10 strawberries

I spy twenty
fluttery things.
They're butterflies
with blue-and-white wings.

Look closer

Let's find a close-up of...

a pig

a sheepdog

a sheep

a tractor

a corn on the cob

some whe

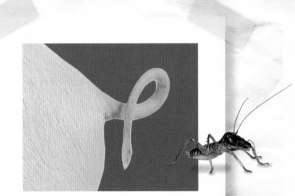

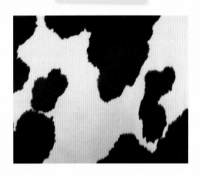

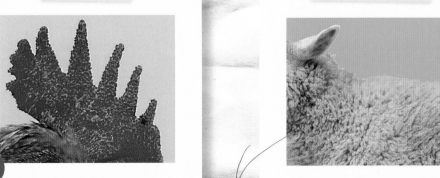

strawberry

a mallard duck

a slice of orange

a sunflower

a wellie boot

a frog

a cat

a reel of string

a cockerel

Now look at these pages one more time, and count the crickets. There are nine!

Farm silhouettes

Let's find silhouettes of...

a flower

4 pears

3 ducklings

a hay bale

2 bananas

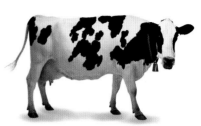
a cow

a calf

130

a chick

a sheepdog

3 snails

a watering can

a rabbit

a basket
of eggs

a lamb

a tractor

3 kittens

2 pots
of yoghurt

I spy a silhouette
that goes
cock-a-doodle-doo!
How quickly
can you find it, too?

131

What goes together?

Let's work out which things go together
by following the dotted lines.

Cows give us…

Wheat is ground up
to make…

Strawberries are
used to make…

flour

strawberry jam

milk

A stable is
a home for a...

chicken

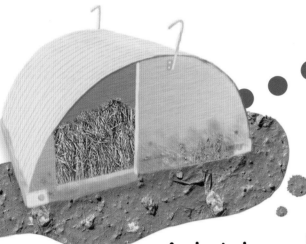

A pigsty is
a home for a...

horse

A chicken coop is
a home for a...

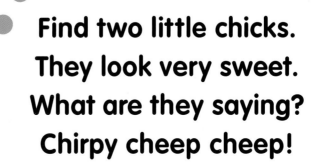

Find two little chicks.
They look very sweet.
What are they saying?
Chirpy cheep cheep!

pig

133

Farm shapes

Let's find...

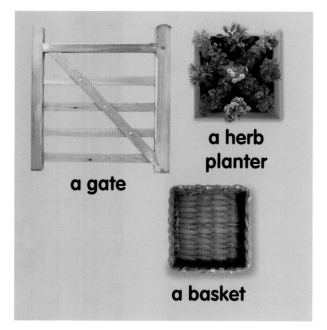

a gate

a herb planter

a basket

squares

a food trough

a fence

a crate of tomatoes

rectangles

a sunflower

a nest

an apple

circles

3 olives

an egg

a lemon

ovals

a duck house   a wedge of cheese

triangles

I spy a slice of starfruit.
It's the shape of a star.
Can you see this fruit?
You won't need
to look far.

135

Farm colours

Let's find...

a yellow sunflower

a blue tractor

a pair of red wellies

3 green leaves

2 pink piglets

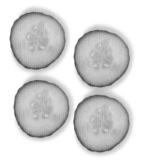
4 green slices
of cucumber

a black tyre

2 white lambs

a yellow chick

a brown foal

an orange slice
of orange

a silver bucket

an orange
carrot

a brown sack
of brown potatoes

a bunch of
green grapes

a brown hen

a blue
watering can

a red strawberry

a purple plum

I can see twelve rainbows,
beautiful and bright.
Let's count them all.
What a colourful sight!

Toy farm

Let's find...

3 horses

a cockere

2 tractors

an owl

a swan

a bucket

a black shee

a pig and 3 piglets

a mallard duck

3 frogs

a kennel

dog with a collar

4 butterflies

2 farmers

a cow

There are five kitty cats for you to seek. Point to the one you would like to keep.

More to find!

You'll find all these things if you go back and look in the busy Farm chapter of this hide-and-seek book!

3 flowers in a pot

a bath duck

2 crates of potatoes

a jar of marmalade

a broccoli floret

a box of lemons

2 chickens at a chicken feeder

a forklift truck

a sleeping toy dog

half a coconut

a hammer

4 kiwi fruits

3 leaping salmon

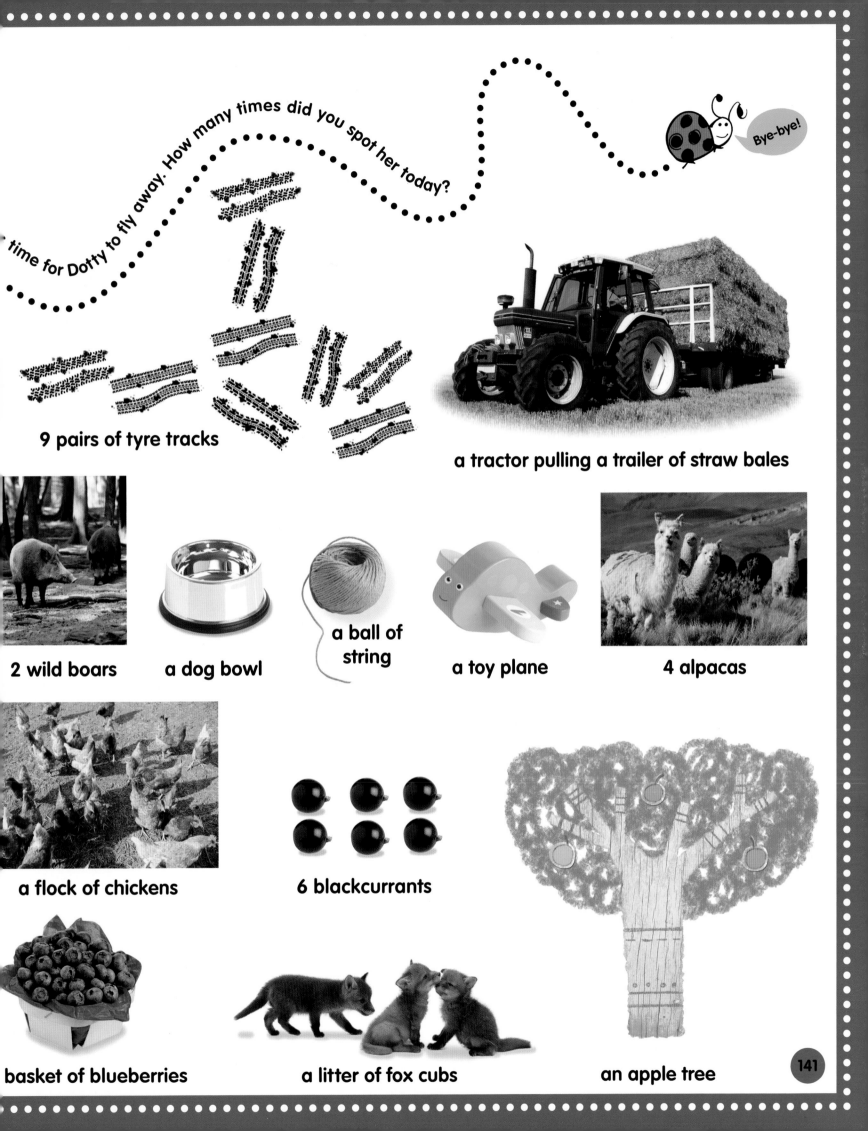

time for Dotty to fly away. How many times did you spot her today?

Bye-bye!

9 pairs of tyre tracks

a tractor pulling a trailer of straw bales

2 wild boars

a dog bowl

a ball of string

a toy plane

4 alpacas

a flock of chickens

6 blackcurrants

basket of blueberries

a litter of fox cubs

an apple tree

things that go

This is Benjie Bus.
He's in every scene of this
chapter. See if you can spot
him again and again!

On the road
Let's find...

2 bicycles

a blue hatchback

a green electric car

a silver saloon

a tow truck

a van

a yellow bus

a motorbike

a four-wheel drive car

a red camper van

2 scooters

an old blue sports car

a caravan

a stretch limousine

an ice cream van

an orange coach

a delivery lorry

a motorized rickshaw

Find the green toy cars.
There are five.
Then choose a vehicle
you'd like to drive.

145

Flying high!

Let's find...

a glider

a fighter pl[ane]

a blue plane

a white triplane

a yellow biplane

a seaplane

a microlight

a red biplane

G-PITZ

a passenger plane

a hot-air balloon

4 helicopters

I spy
flying high
four pink toy planes
in the bright
blue sky.

Floating along

Let's find...

a narrow boat

a cruise ship

a lifeboat

a canoe

a kayak

a speedboat

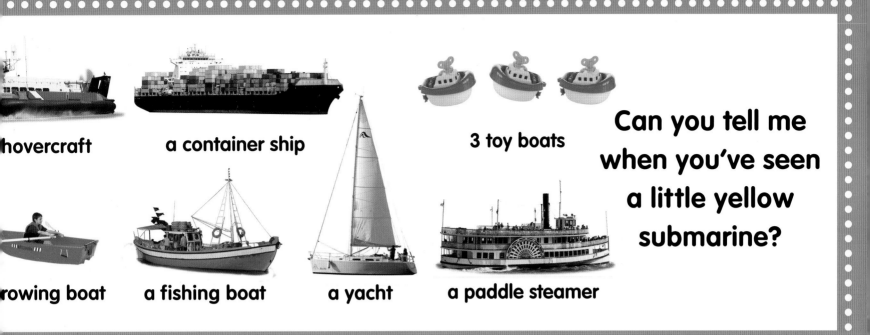

hovercraft

a container ship

3 toy boats

rowing boat

a fishing boat

a yacht

a paddle steamer

Can you tell me when you've seen a little yellow submarine?

Trains and trams
Let's find...

a toy
station

a high-speed
train

a circular
track

a train going over an
arched railway bridge

a toy train

a monorail

a tram

a cable
car

a toy
train tunnel

an underground
train

railway
signals

a funicular
railway

a toy
passenger
carriage

a freight train

4 toy
passengers

an old train
carriage

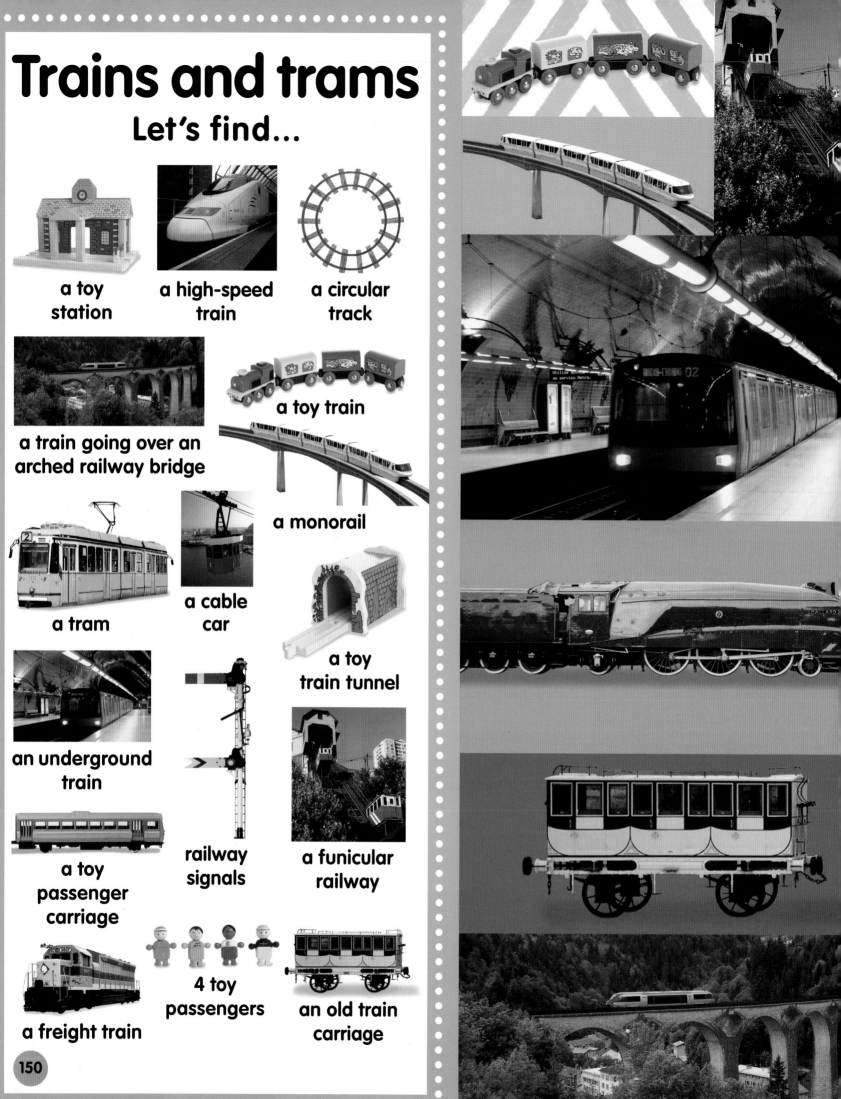

Puffing smoke
and chugging
down the track,
I spy a steam train.
Its engine is black.

151

Tough trucks

Let's find...

a tanker

a yellow-and-white
tipper truck

a white
tipper truck

a white
refrigerator lorr

5 red toy trucks

 green toy
use collector

 a green
pick-up truck

 a yellow
delivery lorry

 a logging
truck

 **Ready steady, good luck! Find the concrete mixer truck.**

 a road sweeper

 a purple tow truck towing a tipper truck

Roll, ride, slide!

Let's find...

a boy on a
balance bike

a pull-along
dog

2 skateboarders

a skier

a boy in a red car

a bicycle with
stabilizers

a dolly
in a pram

a girl in a blue car

a boy
on a scooter

a girl
on a scooter

an ice skater

a push-along
cart

a girl on
in-line skates

Point to the little three-wheeled trike.
Now choose something here that you would like.

154

At the building site

Let's find...

a toy digger

a giant blue tracked excavator

a green dump truck

8 hazard cones

a backhoe loader

3 smiley builders

a forklift truck

a toy roller

a grader

a green wheel loader

a yellow excavator with a drill

I'm sure you won't have any trouble finding a bulldozer clearing rubble!

Emergency!
Let's find...

a fire engine carrying a firefighter

a rescue helicopter

a fire chief's car

a blue warning light

a fire engine with a yellow ladder

a firefighter's helmet

2 stretchers

a police car

an inflatable lifeboat

a police motorbike

a lifeboat

a toy fire station

an ambulance

a medical kit

a torch

an off-road emergency vehicle

a green airport fire engine

Where's the
toy fire engine
with its ladder in the air?
I'm sure it's here.
Do you know where?

159

On the farm
Let's find...

a tractor pulling a plough

a tractor pulling
an empty trailer

a combine harvester

a tractor pulling
a trailer of sugar cane

an all-terrain vehicle

a tractor pulling
a bale maker

a tractor pulling
a grass cutter

a tractor pulling
a manure spreader

a toy tractor

3 bales of straw

a tractor pulling a crop sprayer

an eight-wheeled
tractor

I spy farm animals,
big and small.
There are ten altogether.
Spot them all!

a tractor with
a seed-drill

At the races
Let's find...

3 toy racing cars with toy drivers

a yellow-and-white Formula 1 racing car

a race track

a purple road racing bicycle

Thrust 2, a land-speed racing car

a yellow-and-blue racing motorbike

a time trial bicycle

a Le Mans racing car

a go-kart

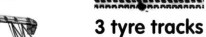
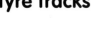

3 tyre tracks

a chequered racing flag

a spanner

a dragster

162

**Rally car number 4
is ready
to race.
But where
oh where
is its hiding place?**

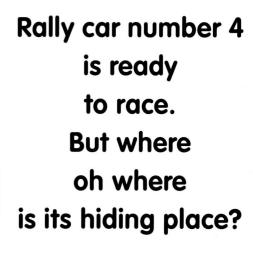

Up in space!
Let's find...

the Viking
spacecraft

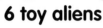
the Lunar 3
satellite

the Apollo 11
Command
Module

the Apollo 11
Command and
Service Module

6 toy aliens

an asteroid

the International
Space Station

the Moon

a comet

the Saturn V
rocket

a waving
astronaut

the Mariner 10
spacecraft

the Discovery
space shuttle

a toy
space buggy

164

Neptune

Moon

Earth

Uranus

Find the planets.
There are eight.
You'll spot them all
because you're great!

Saturn

Jupiter

Venus

Mars

Sun

Mercury

Monster machines!

Let's find...

a giant
tracked excavator

a monster truck

a cruise ship

a tow truck lifting
another tow truck

a mobile
crane

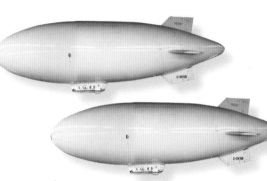

2 airships

a shuttle carrier aircraft
carrying a space shuttle

an Australian
road train

a tandem rotor
heavy-lift helicopter

an amphibious
assault ship

a car transporter

Here's something big for you to spy –
a giant dump truck.
Its back lifts high.

Parts and pieces

Let's find....

a car door

a car seat

a car dashboard

a silver
headlight

a digger
bucket

a windscreen
wiper

a bicycle seat

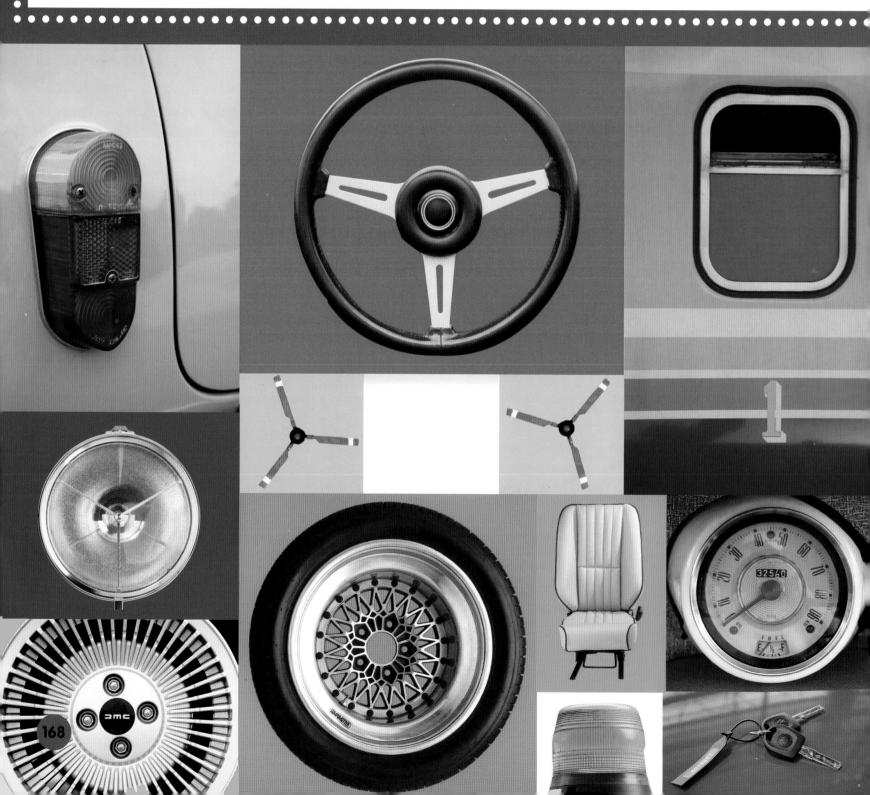

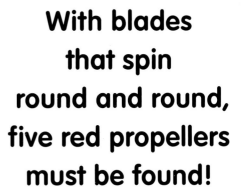

gear stick

a petrol cap

a rear-view mirror

a train window

steering wheels

a tractor windscreen

2 car keys on a key ring

With blades that spin round and round, five red propellers must be found!

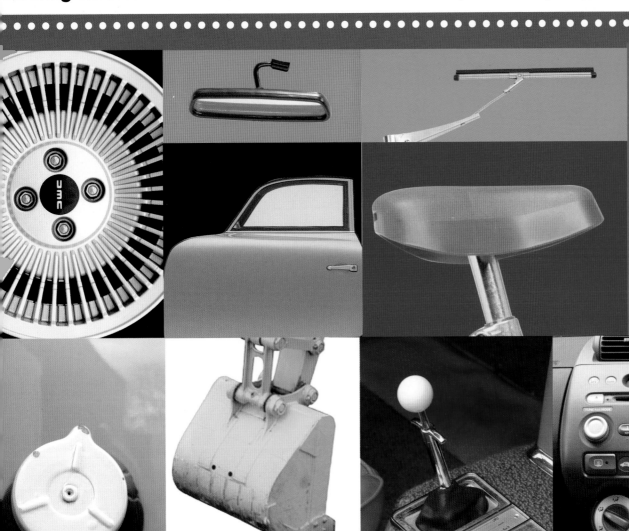

Motor maze!

Let's find out where each vehicle is going by following the dotted lines.

The fire engine is going to a...

The train is going to a...

The van is going to a...

The cyclist is going to a...

shop

park

fire station

beach

170

school

The delivery lorry is
going to a…

he car is going to a…

farm

he bus is going to a…

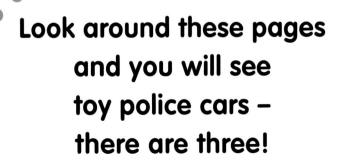

factory

e tractor is going to a…

**Look around these pages
and you will see
toy police cars –
there are three!**

house

Busy counting!

Let's find...

1 plane

2 steam trains

3 helicopters

Lots of
hot-air balloons
flying by.
Can you
count twenty?
Give it a try!

4 fire chief's cars

5 wheel loaders

6 toy ambulances

7 toy tractors

8 toy motorbikes

9 cars

10 toy
sailing boats

Wheels and tracks

Let's find a matching wheel or crawler track for...

a pull-along dog

a tractor

a toy digger

a scooter

a monster truck

an old car

an off-road vehicle

a cardboard bus

an in-line skate

a skateboard

a cannon

a toy roller

a penny-farthing

a toy wrecking ball machine

Where is the caterpillar that can roll and crawl? It has ten wheels. Can you count them all?

175

Super silhouettes

Let's find silhouettes of...

a convertible car

4 anchors

4 hazard cones

an inflatable dinghy with a motor

an off-road emergency vehicle

2 police motorbikes

a fighter plane

176

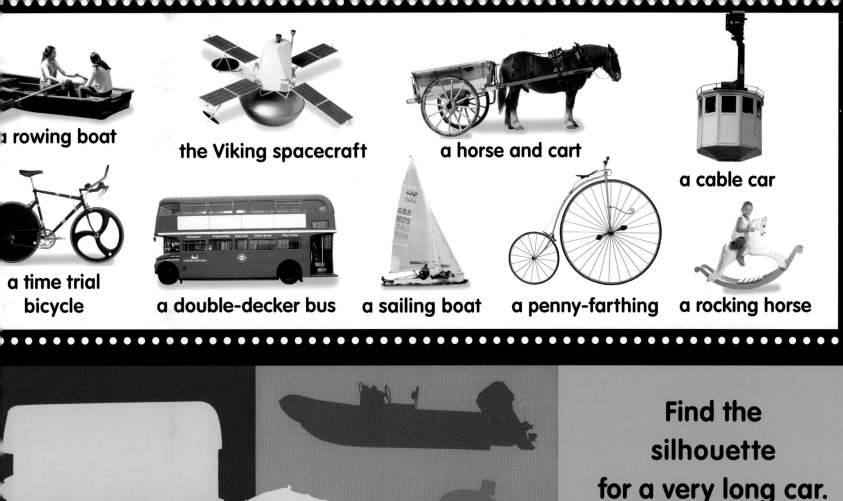

a rowing boat

the Viking spacecraft

a horse and cart

a cable car

a time trial bicycle

a double-decker bus

a sailing boat

a penny-farthing

a rocking horse

Find the silhouette for a very long car. Inside, perhaps there's a superstar!

What goes together?

Let's find the right vehicle for each character by following the dotted lines.

An astronaut flies a...

A police officer drives a...

A firefighter drives a...

A horse is carried in a...

horsebox

fire engine

police car

spacecraft

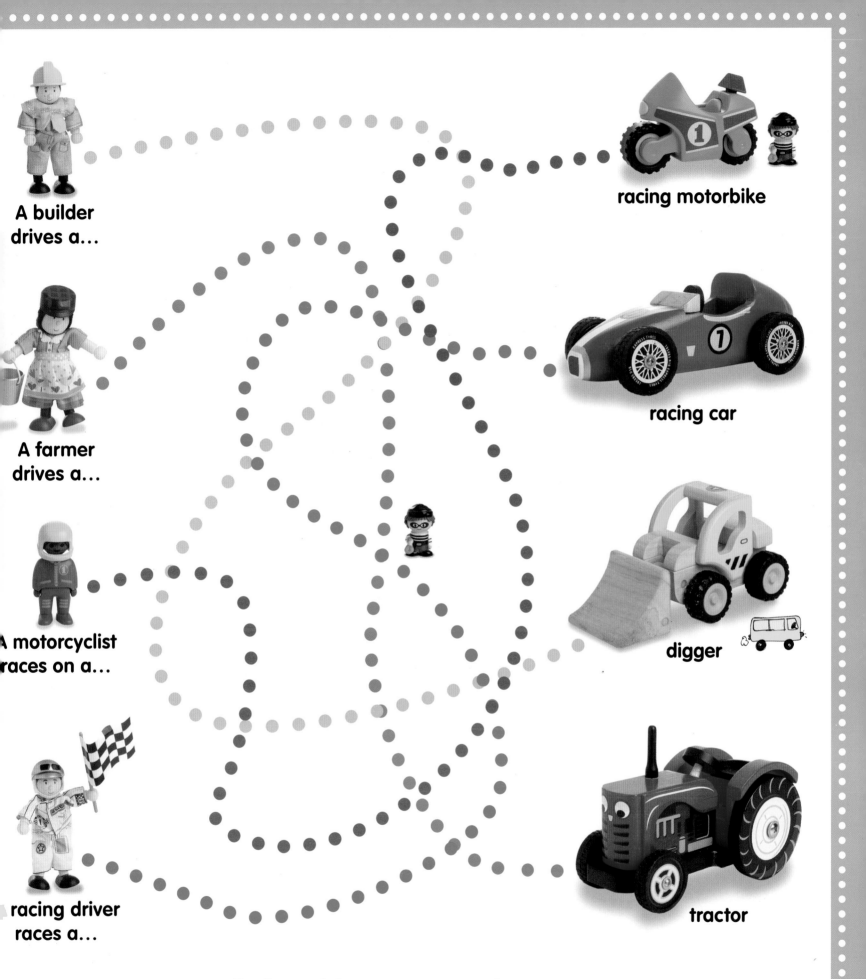

A builder drives a...

A farmer drives a...

A motorcyclist races on a...

racing driver races a...

racing motorbike

racing car

digger

tractor

Four little robbers are getting away.
Let's jump in the police car and find them today!

179

Show me shapes!

Let's find...

a petrol station sign

a chequered racing flag

the double doors of a lorry

a deer sign

squares

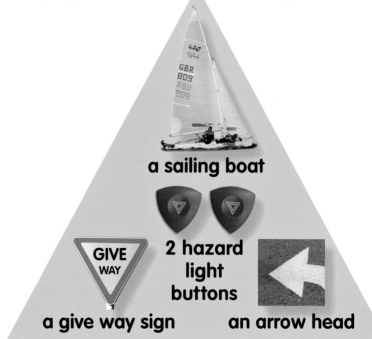

a sailing boat

2 hazard light buttons

GIVE WAY

a give way sign

an arrow head

triangles

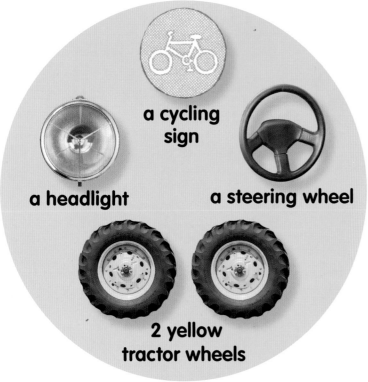

a cycling sign

a headlight

a steering wheel

2 yellow tractor wheels

circles

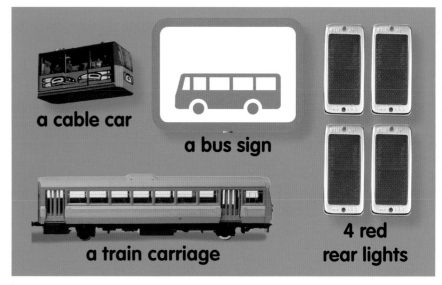

a cable car

a bus sign

a train carriage

4 red rear lights

rectangles

I spy two cars going round a track.
What shape is the track?
Can you tell me that?

GBR 809

470

GIVE WAY

181

Colour fun
Let's find...

3 yellow helicopters

2 red racing cars

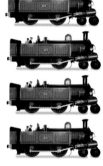

2 white sailing boats

a green motorbike

a blue tractor

a yellow builder's hat

a black tyre

a pink car

2 purple road racing bicycles

an orange logging truck

a white refrigerator lorry

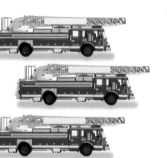

3 red fire engines

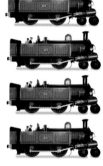

4 brown steam engines

a yellow excavator with a drill

an orange coach

a blue warning light

a green off-road vehicle

a purple hot-air balloon

6 green toy cars

a blue scooter

Where's the toy tractor that's looking at you?
It's red, green, and yellow, and purple, too!

Toy town
Let's find...

a fire engine

a tractor

a yellow
school bus

a forklift
truck

a green
refuse collector

a pink
plane

a pink
ice cream van

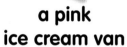
3 pink cars

a road
sweeper

a blue-and-orange
boat

a farm
truck

a camper van

a train

a digger
truck

a truck
transporter

It's a busy day in the toy town.
Spot the helicopter
flying around.

More to find!

You'll find all these things if you go back and look in the last busy chapter of this hide-and-seek book!

a blue tractor with a grapple fork

5 paper planes

an old yellow racing plane

a pull-along ladybird

a blue steam engine

a bicycle bell

an old wooden plane

a white pick-up truck

the Vostok 1 spacecraft

a yellow tow truck

a nurse

a patient

a horn

a waving racing driver

a long-armed loader filling a tipper truck

a blue cabless tract

It's time for Benjie to drive away. How many times did you spot him today?

Bye-bye!

7 hazard barriers

a lighthouse

a doctor

2 rainbow hot-air balloons with empty baskets!

2 kites

2 seagulls

a red toy car with a smiley face

a yellow tracked excavator

a ferry

green-and-yellow toy dump truck

a red toy biplane

a horse and rider

the Sun

a battleship

2 red stars

a jet ski

Index of words we've found!

aardvark 88
abacus 49
accordion 38
aeroplanes 146–147,
166, 172, 176, 181, 184,
186
African bison 72
African elephant 72
airport fire engine 158
airships 166
aliens 164
all-terrain vehicle 110,
160
alligator 66
alpacas 125, 141
ambulances 158, 172
American badger 76
American beaver 64
American crocodile 66
American porcupine 65
amphibious assault
ship 166
anchors 176
angel 46
angelfish 69
animal group names
106–107, 141
animal homes 100, 104,
114, 125, 133, 134, 139
animal noises 98,
116–117, 121, 131, 133
animals 149, 160, 161,
177, 187
ants 60, 72, 76
Apatosaurus 82
Apollo 11 Command
and Service Module
164
Apollo 11 Command
Module 164
apple juice 122
apple orchard 124
apple tart 122
apple tree 49
apple trees 98, 141
apples 112, 124, 134, 141
Arctic hare 79
Arctic tern 89
armadillos 90
armchair 49
arrow head (road sign)
180
Asian elephant 74
asteroid 164
astronauts 164, 178
Australian road train
166
axe 118
Aylesbury ducks 104,
114

baboon 73
baby 14, 15, 34
baby animals 98, 99,
100, 104, 106, 114, 116,
120–121, 126, 130, 131,
133, 136, 139
baby rabbits 80, 106,
121
backhoe loader 28, 156
bags of flour 122, 132
balance bike 154
bald eagles 64
bale maker 160
baler 110
bales of straw
160

ball 6
ballerinas 40
balls of string 119, 141
banana plantation 124
bananas 113, 124, 130
banded sea snakes 68
basket of blueberries
112, 141
basket of cherries 112,
113
basket of eggs 131
basket of logs 118
baskets 112, 113, 118,
131, 134, 141
bat-eared fox 73
bath 34
bath ducks 139, 140
bats 31, 88
battleship 149, 187
baubles 46
beach 170
Beagle 54
bed 14, 15, 34
bee farm 124
beehive 114
bees 2, 60, 114, 116, 117,
124
beetles 60, 74, 86, 92
bells 38, 101
belt 8
beluga whale 68, 78,
95
bicycle bell 181, 186
bicycle seat 168
bicycle with stabilizers
154
bicycles 144, 145, 154,
155, 162, 170, 175,
177, 182
bike 34
billy goat 59, 100
binoculars 20
biplanes 144, 146, 147,
187
bird house 12
birdcage 49
birds 12, 31, 42, 49,
104–105, 106, 114, 116,
120, 121, 126, 129, 130,
131, 133, 136, 138, 139,
140, 141
Birman cat 52
biscuits 26, 122
bison ranch 124
black bear 65
black bull 98, 99
black cat 114
black pig with a pink
stripe 100
black sheep 98, 138
black stallion 102
black steam engine 151
black tyres 108, 136, 182
black-and-white calves
99
black-and-white cows
99, 106, 116, 126, 130,
132
black-faced sheep 98
blackbird 62
blackboard 16
blackcurrants 135, 141
block of butter 122
blue cabless tractor 108
blue cars 144, 154, 162,
172, 179, 181
blue planes 146, 172

blue scooters (motor
vehicles) 144, 182
blue steam engine 150,
186
blue tracked excavators
156, 166
blue tractors 108, 136,
138, 141, 160, 161, 171,
182, 184, 186
blue trailer 108
blue warning lights 158,
182
blue watering can 136
blue-and-orange boat
184
blue-and-white
butterflies 126
blue-ringed octopus 69
blueberries 112, 141
boar (male pig) 100
boars (wild) 125, 141
boats 20, 24, 32,
148–149, 158, 166,
172, 176, 177, 182,
184, 187
bongo drum 38
book 42
bookshelf 48
boots 118, 119, 129, 136
bottles of apple juice
122
bottles of milk 122
bow 18
bow tie 30
bowls 22, 26, 49
box jellyfish 69
box of lemons 113, 140
box of oranges 112
boys (on ride-on toys)
154
bracelet 15, 42
Brachiosaurus 82
bread 122
bride and groom 31
bridge 150
broccoli florets 112, 140
brooch 42
brood of ducklings 106
broom 49, 118
brown cows 98, 99, 120
brown foals 102, 121,
136
brown hens 104, 120,
126, 133, 136, 141
brown nanny goats
100, 116, 120, 126
brown sack of brown
potatoes 113, 136
brown steam engines
182
brown trout 70
brown-and-white
calves 99, 121, 130
bubble bath 32
bubbles 32, 33
buckets 20, 29, 58, 94,
100, 118, 136, 138
buckle 42
budgies 56
bug 14
builder's hat 182
builders 28, 29, 156,
179
building machines
156–157, 166, 172,
174, 175, 179, 182,
184, 186, 187

building site 156–157
bulbs 12
bull 59, 98, 99
bull snake 77
Bulldog 55
bulldozers 28, 156, 157
bunch of bananas 113
bunch of green grapes
112, 113, 136
bunches of herbs 122
bunk bed 34
bus sign 180
buses 3, 14, 24, 144,
145, 171, 175, 177, 184
bushbaby 72
butter 122
butterflies 60, 74, 86,
90, 126, 127, 139
butterfly 12, 14, 32
buttons 8

cable cars 150, 177,
180
cabless tractor 108,
161, 186
caiman 66
cake cases 26
cake slice 48
cake stand 26
cakes 26, 27
calculator 16
calves 99, 121, 130
camera 6
camper vans 144, 184
canary 56
candles 27, 44
candy canes 46
cannon 175
canoe 148
cap 20
car dashboard 168
car keys 169
car seat 168
car transporter 48, 166
caravan 144
cardboard bus 175
cardinal birds 65
carrots 113, 136
cars 6, 7, 24, 48, 144,
145, 154, 158, 162,
163, 166, 171, 172, 176,
178, 179, 180, 181, 182,
184, 187
cart 102
carton of goat's milk
100
carton of milk (cow's)
122
casserole dish 22
castanet 39
cat basket 53, 94
cat collar 54
cat paw prints 54
caterpillars 6, 18, 60,
84, 175
cats 6, 16, 17, 18, 19, 31,
35, 48, 52, 53, 6, 8,
86, 90, 92, 94
cats and kittens 114, 118,
120, 129, 138, 139
cattle 98–99, 106, 116,
120, 121, 124, 126, 130,
132, 139
cattle ranch 124
cauldron 31
centipedes 88
chairs 34, 49

chalk 16
chameleons 66, 74
cheese 100, 122, 134
cheetah 73, 86
chef 49
chequered racing flags
162, 180
cherries 112, 113
chest of drawers 34
chestnut horse 102
chick that has just
hatched 104
chicken coop 133
chicken feeder 140
chickens and chicks
104, 105, 107, 120,
126, 133, 136, 140, 141
chickens at a chicken
feeder 105, 140
chicks 15, 80, 86, 104,
106, 116, 120, 131,
133, 136
Chihuahuas 55
children 16, 34
chilli pepper farm 124
chilli peppers 124, 126
chimpanzee 74
Chinese peacock
butterfly 84, 85
chipmunk 76
Christmas tree 46
circles 15, 134, 150, 180
circular track 150
clock 16, 22, 48
close-ups 128–129
clouds 49, 54, 55, 58,
59, 62, 63, 70, 71, 95
clownfish 69, 92
clutch of chicks 106
coaches 144, 182
coat stand 49
Cocker Spaniel 54
cockerels 36, 58, 104,
116, 129, 130, 131, 138
coconut plantation 124
coconuts 124, 135, 140
coffee plantation 124
coins 42
colander 22
comb 8, 14
combine harvester 110,
160
comet 164
compass 42
computer 34
concrete mixer 48
concrete mixer truck 29,
153
cones 28
container ship 149
convertible car 176
cooker 34
coral 68, 95
coral groupers 69, 92
cormorant 70
corn on the cobs 112, 128
cot 34
cotton plantation 124
cotton reel 49
counting from one to
ten 126–127
counting from one to
twenty 172–173
couple 30, 31
courgettes 113
cowbell 59, 95
cowboys 48

cows 10, 36, 58
cows and calves 98–99,
106, 116, 120, 121, 124,
126, 130, 132, 139
crab 32
crate of herbs 118
crate of tomatoes 134
crates of potatoes 138,
140
crawler tracks 174, 175
crayfish 70
crayons 16
crickets 60, 128, 129
crocodile 6, 10
crop sprayer 160
crop-spraying plane 110
crown 42
cruise ships 148, 166
cucumber 112, 136
cup and saucer 18
curly-haired billy goat
100
cycling sign 180
cyclist 170
cygnets 114
cymbals 38

dachshund 55
Dachshund puppy 80
dad 34
dairy 110
daisies 99
Dalmatian 31
damselflies 70
dashboard 168
deckchair 49
deer 62, 106
deer sign 180
Deinonychus 82
delivery lorries 144, 152,
153, 166, 171, 180, 182,
184
desert iguana 66
dice 19
digger bucket 168
digger truck 184
digger wasp 60
diggers 156, 157, 166,
174, 179, 182, 184, 187
dinghy (inflatable) 176
dinosaur 8, 10, 15, 82
Diplodocus 82, 94
Discovery space shuttle
164
diver 32
doctor 158, 187
dog balls 55, 94
dog bowls 49, 138, 141
dog kennel 54, 55, 94
dog lead 55
dog with a collar 139
doggy rattle 18
dogs 10, 35, 37, 54, 55,
8, 90, 92
dogs and puppies 106,
114, 116, 120, 121, 128,
131, 138, 139, 140
doll 6
dolly in a pram 154
dolphin 20, 84, 85
dominoes 18, 31
donkey 36, 59
donkey carrying a pack
102
donkey foals 102, 120
donkeys and donkey
foals 102–103, 116, 120

doors 168, 180
double-decker bus 177
doves 62, 114
dragon 40
dragonfly 12, 60
dragster 162
dress 8
dressing gown 8
drills 28
drivers 162, 163, 178,
179, 186
drums 6, 38
duck houses 104, 134
ducklings 36, 80, 104,
106, 120, 121, 130
ducks 6, 10, 32, 58
ducks and ducklings
104, 106, 114, 116, 129,
139, 140
dump trucks 3, 156,
166, 167, 185, 187
dung beetles 72, 95
dungarees 8

ear protectors 118
earth (planet) 164
earthworms 60
edmontonia 82
eels 70
eggs 31, 63, 104, 105,
122, 131, 134
eggs in a carton 104,
105, 122
Egyptian goose 78
eight-wheeled tractor
108, 160
electric car 144
electric guitar 38
elephant 6, 10, 86
elephant calf 80
emergency vehicles
158–159, 170, 172, 176,
178, 182, 184
emperor penguin 78
ermine 78
European carp 70
European green lizard
66
ewes and lambs 98,
106, 120, 121, 128
excavators 29, 156, 157,
166, 182, 187
eyepatch 48
eyes 22, 23

factory 171
fairies 41
fairy godmother 41
farm 171
farm animals 160, 161,
177
farm machines 160–161,
171, 172, 174, 178, 179,
182, 183, 184, 186
farm shop 122–123
farm truck 184
farmers 36, 139, 179
farms around the world
124–125
fawn 80
feathers 104
fences 114, 134
ferret 77
ferry 149, 187
fighter planes 146, 176
fire chief's cars 158, 172
fire engines 6, 24,

158–159, 170, 178, 182, 184
fire stations 158, 170
firefighter's helmet 158
firefighters 6, 158, 178
fireflies 60
fish 11, 18, 41, 90, 124, 125, 140
fishing boat 149
fishing net 32
flag 20
flamingo 86
flies 60
flippers 20
floating things 148–149, 158, 166, 172, 176, 177, 182, 184, 187
flock of chickens 107, 141
flock of mallard ducks 106
flock of sheep 106
flour 48, 122, 132
flower 61, 95
flower farm 124
flowers 14, 22, 99, 114, 119, 124, 126, 129, 130, 134, 136, 140
flowers in a pot 119, 140
flying machines 144, 145, 146–147, 158, 164–165, 166, 172, 173, 176, 177, 178, 181, 182, 184, 185, 186, 187
foals 59, 80, 102, 120, 121, 136
fob watch 42
food 100, 104, 105, 112–113, 118, 122–123, 124, 126, 128, 129, 130, 131, 132, 134, 136, 140, 141
food bowls 55
food troughs 100, 101, 134
footballs 16, 31
fork 12, 26, 118
forklift trucks 111, 140, 156, 184
Formula 1 racing car 162
four-wheel drive car 144
fox cubs 80, 107, 120, 141
foxes 64, 76, 78
foxes and fox cubs 107, 114, 115, 120, 141
framed photo 22
freight train 150
frogs 2, 10, 12, 16, 23, 39, 70, 86, 114, 116, 129, 139
fruit 15, 22, 48, 49, 112–113, 124, 126, 129, 130, 132, 134, 135, 140, 141
funicular railway 150

gaggle of geese 106
gallimimus 82
garlic 122
gate 134
gazelle 73
gear stick 169
gecko 66
geese 58
geese and goslings 104, 106, 116, 120
gerbil 56
German Shepherd 54
ghost crabs 69
ghosts 30
giant blue tracked excavators 156, 166

giant dump trucks 156, 166, 167
Gila monster 66
giraffes 10, 72, 89
girls (on ride-on toys) 154
give way sign 180
glass lizard 66
glass slipper 40
glasses 16, 30
glider 16, 146
globe 16
gloves 12, 118
glue pen 16
go-kart 162
goat 37
goat's bell 101
goat's cheese 100
goat's milk 100
goats and kids 100–101, 106, 116, 120, 121, 126
goggles 118
Golden Retriever puppies 81, 94
goldfish 56, 92
goose 104, 106, 116, 120
gorilla 74
goshawk 65
goslings 104, 120
grader 156
grape harvester 110
grapes 112, 113, 124, 136
grapple fork 110, 161, 186
grass cutter 160
grater 22
green airport fire engine 158
green cars 144, 146, 182
green dump truck 156
green eight-wheeled tractor 108
green grapes in a bunch 112, 113, 136
green leaves 136
green motorbikes 144, 179, 182
green off-road vehicles 175, 182
green pick-up truck 153
green slices of cucumber 136
green toy refuse collectors 153, 184
green tractor pulling a blue trailer 108
green tractors 108
green wheel loader 156
green-and-yellow toy dump truck 185, 187
Greenland shark 78
grey horse 102
grey squirrel 64
grizzly bear 64
groundhog 77
guinea fowl 90, 94, 104
guinea pigs 56
guitar 38

hairbrush 8
hairy brown cows 98
half a coconut 135, 140
hammers 29, 119, 140
harmonicas 38
hat 19, 20, 31, 42
hatchback 144
hatching eggs 104, 105
hay bales 109, 110, 130
hazard barriers 156–157, 187
hazard cones 156, 176
hazard light buttons 180
headlights 168, 180

hearts 15, 26, 27, 42
helicopters 24, 146–147, 158, 166, 172, 182, 184, 185
helmets 158, 182
hens 36
hens and chicks 104, 105, 107, 120, 126, 133, 136, 140, 141
herb planter 134
herbs 118, 122, 134
herd of cows 106
herd of deer 106
herd of goats 106
herd of pigs 106
hermit crabs 68
Heterodontosaurus 82
high-speed train 150
highchair 34
hippo 10
hobby horse 6
honey 122, 123
hooded skunk 77
hooks 22
horn 169, 186
horse and carriage 40
horse and cart 102, 177
horse and rider 102, 185, 187
horsebox 110, 178
horses (toys) 178, 185, 187
horses 6, 10, 34, 37, 40, 56
horses and foals 102–103, 107, 116, 120, 121, 124, 125, 126, 133, 136, 138
horseshoes 57, 94, 102
hot-air balloons 24, 145, 147, 172, 173, 182, 185, 187
house 171
houseflies 88
hovercraft 149
hummingbird 62
hyena 73

ice cream 20
ice cream vans 144, 184
ice skater 154
icefish 78
iguanas 66, 67, 95
in-line skates 154, 175
Indian Runner ducks 104
inflatable dinghy 176
inflatable lifeboat 158
insects 90
International Space Station 164

jackal 73
jacket 8
jaguar 74
jam 26
jar of biscuits 122
jar of honey 122, 123
jar of marmalade 123, 140
jars of strawberry jam 122, 132
jay 84, 85
jeep 24
jelly mould 26
jet ski 149, 187
jewels 42
joey 10
jug 22
jumpers 8
Jupiter (planet) 165

kangaroo 10, 88
kayak 148
kazoos 38
kennel 139, 37
kettle 22, 48
keyboard 38
keys 22, 42
kids 37, 81, 95, 100, 121
killer whales 68, 86
king 40
kingfisher 62
kites 20, 146, 155, 187
kittens 52, 80, 86, 116, 118, 120, 131
kitty cats 138, 139
kiwi fruits 135, 140
knife 26
koala 86

labradors 55
ladder 29, 37
ladybirds 3, 12, 60, 86
lambs 59, 80, 98, 116, 121, 126, 131, 136
lamp 34
le Mans racing car 162
leaf 14
leaf insects 60
leaping salmon 125, 140
leaves 136
lemming 78
lemons 48, 113, 134, 140
leopard 18
letter 46, 47
lettuces 113, 126
lifeboats 148, 158
lighthouse 149, 187
lights 158, 168, 180, 182
limousines 144, 176, 177
lion cubs 80
lions 10, 41, 73
lipstick 14
litter of baby rabbits 106
litter of fox cubs 107, 141
litter of piglets 106
litter of puppies 106
litter of rabbits 106
litter of sheepdog puppies 106
loader with a grapple fork 110
loaders 109, 110, 156, 157, 172, 186
loaf of bread 122
locust 60
logging trucks 110, 153, 182
logs 118
long-armed loader 156–157, 186
longfin bannerfish 69
lorries 144, 152–153, 171, 180, 182, 184
lovebirds 56
Lunar 3 satellite 164

macaws 62
machines 108–111, 128, 131, 136, 138, 140, 141
magic wands 40, 41
magician's wand 30
magnet 16
magnifying glass 16
magpies 62
mallards 62, 70, 106, 116, 129, 139
man 13, 14
manure spreader 109, 160
Manx cat 52

marbles 6
mares and foals 102, 120, 121
Mariner 10 spacecraft 164
marmalade 123, 140
Mars (planet) 165
mask 20
medal 57, 95, 102
medical kit 158
Mercury (planet) 165
mermaid 32, 41
mice 10, 14, 30, 31, 36, 37, 114, 116
microlight 147
military machines 146, 149, 166, 175, 176, 187
milk 99, 6, 110, 111, 122, 132
milk churns 37, 99
milk snake 66
milk tanker 110, 111
millipede 60
Miniature Schnauzer 54
mirror 48
mite 60
mittens 19
mobile crane 166
mobile phone 28, 29
mole 76
monkey 31, 42
monorail 150
monster machines 156, 166–167, 174
monster trucks 166, 174
moon 41, 164
moths 60, 86
motorbikes 3, 24, 144, 162, 172, 176, 179, 182
motorcyclist 179
motorized rickshaw 144
mouse 59, 116
mouth 22, 23
muesli 122
mug 22
mum 34
mummy and baby animals (both) 98, 99, 100, 102, 104, 106, 114, 116, 118, 120–121, 126, 130, 131, 133, 136, 139, 141
mushrooms 112

nailbrush 32
nanny goats and kids 100, 106, 116, 120, 121, 126
narrow boat 148
narwhal 78
Neptune (planet) 164
nest 134
newt 70
noises 99, 116–117, 121, 131, 133
notebook 16, 19
numbers 24, 25, 44, 45
nurse 159, 186

Ocean sunfish 68
off-road vehicles 110, 158, 175, 176, 182
old cars 144, 174
old machines 144, 146, 147, 150, 151, 174, 175, 177, 182, 186
old planes 146–147, 186
old red tractor 109
old train carriage 150
olives 134
onion 113

orang-utan 74
orange carrots 113, 136
orange coaches 144, 182
orange logging truck 182
orange slices of orange 129, 136
orange tractor pulling a manure spreader 109
orange tractors 109
oranges (fruit) 48, 112, 129, 136
orchard 124
ostriches 62, 88, 95
otter 70
ovals 134
oven glove 26
owl chicks 80
owlet 121
owls 46, 65, 77, 78
owls and owlets 114, 116, 120, 121, 138

paddle steamer 149
paint 16
paint palette 16
paintbrushes 14, 16
painting 16
pair of ear protectors 118
pair of goggles 118
pair of red wellies 136
pair of sparkly shoes 3
pairs of gloves 118
pairs of tyre tracks 111, 141
pairs of wellies 118, 119, 136
panda 30, 90
pants 8
paper planes 146, 147, 181, 186
park 170
parrots 42, 56
passenger carriages 150, 170, 180
passenger plane 147
passenger trains 150, 170, 180
passengers 150
pasta shapes 26
pastry cutter 26
patient 159, 186
paver 29
paw prints 57, 94
pears 130
pebbles 20
pen 16, 42
pencil case 16
pencil sharpener 16
pencils 16, 19
penguin 6, 46
penguin chicks 80
penny-farthings 175, 177
Pentaceratops 82
people 6
Persian cat 52
petrol cap 169
petrol station sign 180
pheasant 104
photo 22
piano 30
pick-up truck 110, 153
pickaxe 29
pig in a pigsty 100
pig's trough 100, 101
piglets 37, 59, 80, 100, 106, 120, 126, 136, 139
pigs 10, 37, 58, 92
pigs and piglets 100–101, 106, 116, 120, 128, 133, 139
pigsties 37, 100, 133

pinecones 46
pink cars 182, 184
pink daisies 99
pink ice cream van 184
pink piglets 100, 106, 120, 126, 136, 139
pink toy planes 146, 147, 184
pink tractor 109
piranhas 74
pirate ship 42
pirate skull 48
pirate's hat 42
pirates 42
pitchfork 37
planes 24, 110, 138, 141, 146–147, 166, 172, 176, 181, 184, 186
planets 44, 164–165
plant pot 12
plantations 124
planter 134
plate 19
plough 160
ploughs 107, 108
plum 136
pocket mouse 76
poison dart frog 74
polar bears 30, 78, 79, 95
police cars 158, 170, 171, 178, 179
police motorbikes 158, 176
police officer 178
police vehicles 158–159, 170, 171, 176, 178, 179
Pomeranian 54
pony 56
Poodle 54
porcupines 73, 89
potatoes 113, 136, 138, 140
pots of yoghurt 122, 131
prairie dog 76
prams 34, 154
present 18
prince 41
princesses 41
propellers 168, 169
puffin 62, 88
Pug 54
pull-along caterpillar 175
pull-along dogs 154, 174
pull-along ladybird 155, 186
pumpkin 112
puppies 55, 56, 80, 81, 94, 106, 121
purple 136
purple hot-air balloon 182
purple plum 136
purple road racing bicycles 162, 182
purple tow trucks 153, 166
purse 19
push-along cart 154
pyjamas 8

queen 40
quill pen 42

rabbit hutch 34
rabbits 10, 30, 35, 56, 65, 77, 79, 89, 90
rabbits and baby rabbits 106, 114, 120, 121, 131
race runner 77
race tracks 162, 180, 181

racing bicycles 162, 177, 182
racing cars 162, 163, 179, 180, 181, 182
racing drivers 163, 179, 186
racing flags 162, 180
racing machines 146–147, 162–163, 177, 179, 180, 181, 182, 186
racing motorbikes 162, 179
racing planes 146–147, 186
racoon 64
railway bridge 150
railway signals 150
railways 150–151
rainbow hot-air balloons 145, 185, 187
rainbow lorikeet 62
rainbows 19, 44, 136, 137
raincoat 8
raisins 26
rake 12, 118
rally car 163
ram 99
ranches 124
rat snakes 65, 66
rattle 18
rear lights 180
rear-view mirror 169
recorder 38
rectangles 15, 180, 134
red biplanes 144, 147, 187
red camper van 144
red cars 154, 158, 162, 171, 172, 176, 182, 184, 187
red cherries in a basket 112, 113
red fire engines 158, 159, 170, 178, 182, 184
red propellers 168, 169
red rear lights 180
red stars 165, 167, 187
red strawberry 136
red toy trucks 152
red tractor pulling a plough 108
red tractor with a loader 109
red tractors 108, 109, 128, 131, 138
red-eyed tree frog 74
reel of string 129
refrigerator lorries 152, 182
refuse collectors 153, 184
reindeer 46
reindeers 78, 92
rescue helicopters 158, 172, 182
rescue machines 144, 152, 153, 158–159, 166, 170, 172, 176, 178, 182, 184, 186
rhinoceros 89
rice farm 124
rice harvester 110
rickshaw 144
ride-on toys 154–155, 177
rider 46, 102
riding hat 102
ring 20, 42, 49
ring-tailed lemur 84, 85
road racing bicycles 162, 182
road sweepers 153, 184
road train 166

robbers 178, 179
robot 6
rocket 6, 164
rocking horse 34, 177
rollers 29, 156, 175
rolling pin 26
rope 118
rosettes 102, 103
rowing boats 149, 177
rubber 16
rubber ring 3, 20
rubbish truck 24
ruler 16

Sack of potatoes 113, 136
sacks 113, 118, 136
saddles 102
sailing boats 149, 172, 177, 180, 182
salmon 70, 125, 140
salmon farm 124
saloon 144
Saltasaurus 82
sandals 20
sandcastle 20
Santa 46
satellite 164
Saturn (planet) 165
Saturn V rocket 164
saucepans 22, 34
sausages 122
saws 29, 118
saxophone 48
scarecrow 58, 95, 114
scarf 8
school 171
school bus 184
scissors 16
scooters (motor vehicles) 24, 144, 182
scooters (ride-on toys) 154, 174
scorpion 89
scroll 42
sea lion 88
sea turtles 68
seagulls 149, 187
seahorses 32, 68, 92
seal pup 80
seals 32, 78, 84, 85
seaplane 146
seats 168
secretary birds 73
seed-drill 160
seeds 49
serving spoon 22
shakers 38
shampoo 32
shapes 134–135, 180–181
sharks 89
shed 118–119
sheep 36, 58
sheep and lambs 98–99, 106, 116, 120, 121, 126, 128, 131, 136, 138
sheepdog puppies 106, 121
sheepdogs and puppies 106, 114, 116, 120, 121, 128, 131
Shi tzu 55
ships 148–149, 166, 187
shire horses 102
shoes 8, 20, 30, 40
shop 170
short-haired brown cows 99, 120
shovel 117
shower 34
shuttle carrier aircraft 166

Siamese cat 52
sieve 22
signs 180
silhouettes 130–131, 176–177
silver bucket 136
silver headlights 168, 180
silver saloon 144
sink 34
skateboarders 154
skateboards 48, 154, 175
skates 154, 175
skeleton 31
skid-steer loader 110
skier 154
skipping rope 16
skirt 8
sledge 46
sleeping toy dogs 138, 140
sleepyhead 14, 15
slice of orange 48
slice of starfruit 134, 135
slice of watermelon 112
slices of cucumber 112, 136
slices of orange 129, 136
slippers 8
sloth 74
slugs 60
smiley builders 156
snails 6, 12, 60, 90, 92, 114, 131
snakes 10, 84, 86, 88, 90, 94
snorkel 20
snowflakes 78, 79, 95
snowmen 46
soap 32
soap dish 32
socks 8
sofa 34
sows and piglets 100, 120
space buggy 164
space machines 164–165, 166, 177, 178, 186
space shuttles 164, 166
space station 164
spacecraft 164–165, 166, 177, 178, 186
spade 20, 118
spanner 118, 162
spatula 22, 48
speedboat 148
Sphynx cat 52
spider hunting wasp 60
spiders 10, 12, 60, 74, 93
spinning top 3, 6
sponge 22, 23, 49
spoonbill 62
spoons 22, 26
sports car 144
spotty pigs 100, 116, 133
squares 15, 134, 180
squirrel 76, 89, 114
stables 125, 133
stacked tyres 108
stacking cups 6
stag beetles 60
stallion 102
stapler 16
starfish 32, 42, 68
starfruit 134, 135
stars 15, 16, 44, 46, 134, 135, 164, 165, 167, 187
station (train) 150
steam engines 150, 151, 172, 182, 186
steam trains 150, 151,

172, 182, 186
steering wheels 169, 180
Stegosaurus 82, 92
stick insects 56
sticklebacks 71
stocking 46
straw bales 109, 141
strawberries 15, 113, 126, 129, 132, 136
strawberry jam 122, 132
stretch limousines 144, 176, 177
stretchers 158
string 12, 119, 129, 141
string of garlic 122
strings of sausages 122
striped skunk 65
stud farm 124, 125
submarine 149
sugar cane plantation 124
Sun 165, 187
sunflowers 12, 114, 129, 134, 136
sunglasses 20
suns 49
superhero 41
swallow 62
swans 62, 70, 138
sweets 46, 49
swimming costume 20
swimming trunks 20
sword 42

T-rex 83
table 34
tambourine 38
tandem rotor heavy-lift helicopter 166
tankers 110, 111, 152
tarantula 74
tea plantation 124
tea towel 22
team of horses 107
teddy 6, 8, 9, 19, 46
telescope 42
television 34
terrapin 56
Thai water dragon 66
thorn bug 60
three-wheeled trike 154, 155
Thrust 2 (land-speed car) 162
tigers 19, 74, 86, 92
tights 48
time trial bicycles 162, 177
tipper trucks 28, 152, 153, 156, 186
tissues 22
toad 70
toadstools 18, 64, 65, 94
toaster 34
toilet 34
tomatoes 48, 113, 134
tongs 22
tool boxes 29, 118
tools 118, 119, 140
toothbrushes 32
torch 49, 158
tortoises 56, 66
toucan 74, 86
tow trucks 144, 152, 153, 166, 186
towel 32
tower 6, 29, 40
triangles 15, 38, 134, 180
toy aliens 164
toy ambulances 172
toy animals 154, 155, 174, 175, 177, 178, 185, 186, 187

toy boats 149, 172, 184
toy cars 144, 145, 154, 162, 170, 171, 178, 179, 182, 184, 187
toy cat 54
toy diggers 156, 174, 179, 184
toy dog 55
toy dogs 138, 139, 140
toy drivers 162, 178, 179
toy fire engines 158, 159, 178, 184
toy fire station 158
toy mice 52
toy motorbikes 172, 179
toy passengers 150
toy planes 138, 141, 144, 146, 147, 184, 187
toy refuse collectors 153, 184
toy rollers 156, 175
toy space buggy 164
toy station (train) 150
toy tractors 109, 138, 160, 172, 179, 182, 183, 184
toy train tunnel 150
toy trains 150, 180, 184
toy trucks 152, 153, 184, 185, 187
toy wrecking ball machine 175
toys 109, 138–139, 140, 141
tracked excavators 156, 157, 166, 182, 187
tracks (crawler tracks) 174, 175
tracks (train) 150–151
tractor lifting a hay bale 109
tractor pulling a trailer of straw bales 109, 141
tractor windscreen 169
tractor with a bale loader 109
tractor with a loader 109
tractors 24, 36, 48, 58, 95, 108–109, 128, 131, 136, 138, 141, 160–161, 169, 171, 172, 174, 179, 180, 182, 183, 184, 186
traffic signs 180
trailer carrying hay bales 110
trailer carrying straw bales 109, 141
trailers 108, 109, 110, 141, 160, 178
train carriages 150, 180
train tunnel 150
train window 169
trainers 8
trains 6, 34, 150–151, 170, 172, 180, 182, 184, 186
trams 150, 151
transporters 166, 184
tray 22
tray of courgettes 113
treasure chest 42
treasure map 42
tree frog 92
trees 46, 49
triangles 15, 38, 134, 180
Triceratops 82
trike 154, 155
triplane 146
Troodon 82
troughs 100, 101, 134
trousers 8
trowel 12
truck transporter 184

trucks 24, 28, 29, 110, 111, 140, 144, 152–153, 156, 157, 166, 167, 171, 174, 182, 184, 185, 186, 187
trumpet 38
tub of muesli 122
tunnel 150
turkey 37, 104
turtle 20, 21
turtles 67
tyre tracks 111, 141, 162
tyres 37, 108, 136, 182

Umbrella 8
underground train 150
Uranus (planet) 165

Vans 144, 170, 184
vegetable peeler 22
vegetables 37, 112–113, 126, 140
vehicle parts 168–169, 174–175, 180, 181, 186
vehicles 108–111, 128, 131, 136, 138, 140, 141
velociraptor 82
Venus (planet) 165
vest 8
Viking spacecraft 164, 177
vineyard 124
volcano 82, 94
Vostok 1 spacecraft 165, 186
vulture 62

Walrus 78
warbler 89
warning lights 158, 182
warships 149, 166, 187
warthog 73
washing-up brush 22
wasp 60
watch 8, 42
water vole 70
watering can 12, 13, 131, 136
watermelon 112
waving astronaut 164
waving racing driver 163, 186
weasel 65
wedges of cheese 122, 134
weighing scale 26
wellie boots 118, 119, 129, 136
wellies 12
western diamondback rattlesnake 66
wheat 49, 128, 132
wheel loaders 28, 156, 172
wheelbarrow 29, 118
wheels 30, 174–175, 180, 182
whisk 26
whistle 49
white Aylesbury duck 104, 114
white horse 102
white horse with brown spots 102, 126, 133
white lambs 98, 116, 121, 126, 131, 136
white pick-up truck 144, 186
white refrigerator lorries 152, 182
white rhinoceros 73
white sailing boats 149,

177, 180, 182
white shire horses 102
white tipper truck 152
white triplane 146
wild boars 65, 125, 141
windmill 20
windows 34
windscreen 169
windscreen wiper 168
witch 41
witch's cat 40
wizard 40
wolf 78
wolverine 78
wooden plane 146–147, 186
wooden spoon 26
woodlice 60
woodpecker 62
world farms 124–125
worms 77
wrecking ball machine 175

Xylophone 38

Yacht 149
yellow builder's hat 182
yellow buses 144, 171, 175, 184
yellow chicks 104, 116, 120, 131, 133, 136
yellow delivery lorries 153, 171
yellow ducklings 104, 106, 120, 121, 130
yellow excavators 156, 157, 182, 187
yellow feathers 104
yellow helicopters 147, 158, 172, 182, 184, 185
yellow planes 146–147, 186
yellow submarine 149
yellow sunflowers 114, 129, 134, 136
yellow tow truck 152, 186
yellow tractor wheels 180
yellow-and-blue racing motorbike 162
yellow-and-white Formula 1 racing car 162
yellow-and-white tipper truck 152
yoghurt 122, 131

Zebras 10, 86, 72, 92

acknowledgements

PICTURE CREDITS

The publisher would like to thank the following for their kind permission to reproduce their photographs:

(Key: a-above; b-below/bottom; c-centre; f-far; l-left; r-right; t-top)

Contents

All images © Dorling Kindersley

First words chapter

All images © Dorling Kindersley

Animals chapter

52 Warren Photographic Limited: Jane Burton (ftl, cb, fcl, bl); Mark Taylor (fbl). **53 Dorling Kindersley:** Rachael Parfitt (fcla/frog aw). **Warren Photographic Limited:** Jane Burton (ftl, tl, c, cr); Kim Taylor (cra); Mark Taylor (fcrb). **54 Alamy Images:** Erik Lam (c/jack russell). **Dorling Kindersley:** Rachael Parfitt (c/frog aw). **Fotolia:** Eric Isselée (cr/border collie). **iStockphoto.com:** Mehmet Salih Guler (cl/doberman); Eric Isselée (fbl/jack russell). **Warren Photographic Limited:** Jane Burton (tc/pomeranian, tc/schnauzer, bl, tr/pugzu, fcra/spaniel, fcr, ftl, fbr, cr/pugzu, fclb/shih tzu, crb/shih tzu, cb/boxer); Mark Taylor (fcl/yorkie, tl, ftr/poodle, crb/yorkie, br). **55 Fotolia:** Eric Isselée (fbr/bull terrier); Michael Pettigrew (c). **Warren Photographic Limited:** Jane Burton (1/fcla/bulldog, 2/fcla/bulldog, 3/fcla/bulldog, 1/ftl/dachshunds, tl/dachshunds, 1/ca/shih tzu, 2/ca/shih tzu, 1/cra/chihuahua, 2/cra/chihuahua, clb/spaniel, clb/chihuahua, bl/schnauzer, cb/bulldog pup, crb/bulldog, bc/pomeranian, fbr/dachshund, fcrb/bulldog pup); Mark Taylor (fcl/poodle, 1/tc/labrador, 2/tc/labrador, cb/labrador, c/beagle). **56 Alamy Images:** Peter Titmuss (bc/horse). **Corbis:** Don Mason (fclb/dog, crb/dog). **Dorling Kindersley:** Rachael Parfitt (fcra/frog aw). **Warren Photographic Limited:** (cl/cats, 1/fcl/stick insect, tl/rabbits, ftl/parrots, tr, fcl/tortoise, tc/dog, cra, 2/ca/goldfish, 1/ca/goldfish, 2/fcl/stick insect, bl/budgerigars, ftr, fcr). **57 Alamy Images:** Peter Titmuss (cl). **Getty Images:** Koki Iino (cr/mouse). **Warren Photographic Limited:** (cra, cr/chinchilla, ftl, fcla, fcrb/cats, fcr, 1/bc/stick insect, 2/bc/stick insect, br, fbr). **58 Corbis:** Ocean (tr). **Dorling Kindersley:** South of England Rare Breeds Centre, Ashford, Kent (1/tl/goose, clb/goose, crb/ducks). **iStockphoto.com:** Bjorn Heller (c/tractor). **Warren Photographic Limited:** (bc/ducklings). **59 Corbis:** Ocean (br/cow). **Dorling Kindersley:** Rachael Parfitt (fcl/frog aw). **Warren Photographic Limited:** (clb/goat); Jane Burton (c). **60 Dorling Kindersley:** Natural History Museum, London (tc, 1/cra/butterfly, 2/cra/butterfly, 3/cra/butterfly, fcl/moth); Natural History Museum, London (fcra/bug). **Getty Images:** Brand X Pictures (1/fcrb/firefly, 2/fcrb/firefly, 3/fcrb/firefly, 4/fcrb/firefly, 5/fcrb/firefly, 6/fcrb/firefly). **61 Dorling Kindersley:** Natural History Museum, London (c/millipede, ftl/butterfly, fcr/butterfly, fbl/butterfly, tc/moth); Natural History Museum, London (c/red bug, fclb/beetle); Rachael Parfitt (cr/frog aw). **Getty Images:** Brand X Pictures (ftl/firefly, tr/firefly, fcra/firefly, c/firefly, clb/firefly, fcrb/firefly, fbr/firefly). **62 Fotolia:** Steve Byland (1/bl/swan, 2/bl/swan, 3/bl/swan, cra/swan, ftr); Eric Isselée (tc/vulture). **iStockphoto.com:** Robert Blanchard (clb/spoonbill); Thomas Sztanek (fcl/lorikeet); Karel Broz (1/ftl/macaw, 2/ftl/macaw, fcr); Cay-Uwe Kulzer (fcla/woodpecker); Nicola Destefano (cb/turtledove); Andrew Howe (1/c/magpie, cla/blackbird, tr/swift, 2/c/magpie, fclb/swallow, bc/kingfisher, fcra/swallow); Paul Tessier (ca/mallard, tl/puffin, cl/hummingbird, cr). **63 Dorling Kindersley:** Rachael Parfitt (fbl/frog aw). **Fotolia:** Steve Byland (ftl/swan); Eric Isselée (tl/vulture). **iStockphoto.com:** Robert Blanchard (cra/spoonbill); Shunyu Fan (clb/nest); Andrew Howe (cla/tit, fcl/wren, tc/swift, fcra/swift, fcla/magpie, cb/tit, c/magpie, fcl/tit, c/kingfisher, cla/robin, fcl/robin, clb/blackbird); Karel Broz (fcla/macaw); Thomas Sztanek (fcr/lorikeet); Paul Tessier (fbr/mallard, bc); Nicola Destefano (fclb/turtledove); Cay-Uwe Kulzer (c/woodpecker). **64 Dorling Kindersley:** Rachael Parfitt (fcr/frog aw). **Getty Images:** First Light / Ken Gillespie (cra); Photodisc / Life On White (bl); Photodisc / Martin Harvey (ftr); Photodisc / Sylvain Cordier (1/fcla/eagle); Flickr / Bucks Wildlife Photography (2/fcla/eagle); Stone+ / Catherine Ledner (tr); Flickr / Bill Wakeley Photography (cr/bird, cl); The Image Bank / Winfried Wisniewski (fcl); Workbook Stock / Tier Und Naturfotografie J & C Sohns (fclb/porcupine); Taxi / Giel (cb); Photonica / Tariq Dajani (crb). **Lonely Planet Images:** Holger Leue / Lonely Planet Images (ca/bear). **Warren Photographic Limited:** Jane Burton (1/ca/fox, 2/ca/fox, c/fox, 1/clb/rabbit, 2/clb/rabbit, 1/fbr/rabbit, 2/fbr/rabbit, fcr); Kim Taylor (cla/squirrel, cr/squirrel, fcr/bat); Mark Taylor (fcra). **65 Getty Images:** First Light / Ken Gillespie (crb); Photodisc / Life On White (ftl/skunk); The Image Bank / Winfried Wisniewski (fcla/goshawk); Taxi / Giel (tl/bear); Workbook Stock / Tier Und Naturfotografie J & C Sohns (tc/porcupine); Photodisc / Sylvain Cordier (c/eagle); Flickr / Bill Wakeley Photography (1/cra/cardinal, 2/cra/cardinal, 3/cra/cardinal, fcr/cardinal); Photonica / Tariq Dajani (fcra); National Geographic / Joel Sartore (fcl); Flickr / Bucks Wildlife Photography (fcr/eagle); Photodisc / Martin Harvey (fcrb/raccoon); Stone+ / Catherine Ledner (fbr). **Lonely Planet Images:** Holger Leue / Lonely Planet Images (bl). **Photolibrary:** Martyn Chillmaid / Oxford Scientific (OSF) (ca/snake, c/snake). **Warren Photographic Limited:** Jane Burton (1/ca/rabbit, 2/ca/rabbit, 3/ca/rabbit, 4/ca/rabbit, 5/ca/rabbit, 6/ca/rabbit, fcrb/rabbit, br); Kim Taylor (cr/bat); Mark Taylor (clb). **66 FLPA:** Michael & Patricia Fogden / Minden Pictures (fcrb); Tom Vezo / Minden Pictures (c/gila, fbr). **Getty Images:** Gallo Images / Heinrich Van Den Berg (ca); Riser / JH Pete Carmichael (ftr); The Image Bank / Darrin Klimek (cr, fbl/snake); Photographer's Choice / Cristian Baitg (c/chameleon); Photolibrary / Stan Osolinski (tl); Gallo Images / Roger de la Harpe (clb); National Geographic / Joel Sartore (cl/glass lizard); Visuals Unlimited / Joe McDonald (fcra); The Image Bank / Joseph Devenney (bl, cra); Robert Harding World Imagery / James Hager (ftl, crb); Science Faction / Chip Simons (fbl, br). **67 Dorling Kindersley:** Rachael Parfitt (c/frog aw). **FLPA:** Sebastian Kennerknecht / Minden Pictures (bc); Cyril Ruoso / Minden Pictures (fcrb); Heidi & Hans-Juergen Koch / Minden Pictures (ca). **Getty Images:** Flickr / Rick Poon (fbr); Riser / JH Pete Carmichael (fcl); Riser / Kevin Schafer (fclb); Photonica / Zac Macaulay (cra/turtle); Gallo Images / Heinrich Van Den Berg (fcra); Gallo Images / Roger de la Harpe (cl); Photographer's Choice / Cristian Baitg (c); Photolibrary / Stan Osolinski (cr); National Geographic / Joel Sartore (fbl); Workbook Stock / David Maitland (cb). **68 Corbis:** Hal Beral (cb/grouper fish); Robert Llewellyn (1/tr/starfish, 2/tr/starfish, 3/tr/starfish, 4/tr/starfish, 5/tr/starfish, fbl/starfish, bl/starfish, br/starfish); Frans Lanting (cl); Martin Harvey (1/fcr/striped fish, 2/fcr/striped fish, 3/fcr/striped fish, 4/fcr/striped fish, 5/fcr/striped fish); Winfried Wisniewski / Zefa (fbr/crab). **Dorling Kindersley:** Jeremy Hunt - modelmaker (cr/shark); David Peart (1/tc/turtle, 2/tc/turtle, cla/turtle, ca); Weymouth Sea Life Centre (c/octopus); Natural History Museum, London (1/bc/shell, 2/bc/shell). **imagequestmarine.com:** (1/ftr/sea krait, 2/ftr/sea krait, cb/sea krait). **Photolibrary:** Juniors Bildarchiv (tr/killer whale). **SeaPics.com:** (ftr/sunfish). **69 Corbis:** Hal Beral (1/tl/grouper fish, 2/tl/grouper fish, clb/grouper fish); Robert Llewellyn (fbl/starfish, fbr/starfish); Martin Harvey (1/fcl/striped fish, 2/fcl/striped fish, 3/fcl/striped fish, 4/fcl/striped fish, 1/fcla/striped fish, 2/fcla/striped fish, 3/fcla/striped fish, 4/fcla/striped fish, 5/fcla/striped fish, 6/fcla/striped fish, 7/fcla/striped fish, 8/fcla/striped fish, 9/fcla/striped fish, 10/fcla/striped fish, fbr/striped fish); Winfried Wisniewski / Zefa (fbl/crab, 1/tc/crab, 2/tc/crab); Norbert Wu / Science Faction (1/ca/jellyfish, 2/ca/jellyfish, 3/ca/jellyfish, 4/ca/jellyfish, 1/cl/jellyfish, 2/cl/jellyfish, 3/cl/jellyfish, 4/cl/jellyfish). **Dorling Kindersley:** Natural History Museum, London (fbl/shell, br/shell); Weymouth Sea Life Centre (cla); Rachael Parfitt (fbr/frog aw). **imagequestmarine.com:** (crb/sea krait). **Photolibrary:** Juniors Bildarchiv (cr/killer whale). **SeaPics.com:** (c/sunfish). **70 FLPA:** Flip De Nooyer / FN / Minden (cl/otter, fcl/cormorant). **Getty Images:** Botanica / Picavet (1/ftl/eel, 2/ftl/eel, 3/ftl/eel, cr/eel); Photolibrary / Robin Redfern (fclb/vole); Riser / GK Hart / Vikki Hart (4/tc/ducks, fcra); First Light / Thomas Kitchin & Victoria Hurst (1/fcl/salmon, 2/fcl/salmon, 3/fcl/salmon, 4/fcl/salmon, fcrb); First Light / Doug Hamilton (1/tc/duck, 2/tc/duck, 3/tc/duck); Lifesize / Don Farrall (1/clb/frog, 2/clb/frog); Stone / Paul Taylor (1/fcla/damselfly, 2/fcla/damselfly, tr); Stock Image / Frank Lukasseck (ftr). **71 Dorling Kindersley:** Rachael Parfitt (fbr/frog aw). **FLPA:** Flip De Nooyer / FN / Minden (ftr/otter, tr/cormorant). **Getty Images:** Botanica / Picavet (clb/eel, cb/eel); Gallo Images / Heinrich van den Berg (c/moorhen); Stone / Paul Taylor (ftr/damselfly); First Light / Thomas Kitchin & Victoria Hurst (fcl, clb/salmon, crb); First Light / Doug Hamilton (cla/duck, ca/duck, tc/duck); Lifesize / Don Farrall (cra/frog, fcr/frog); Photolibrary / Robin Redfern (fcr/vole). **72 Dorling Kindersley:** Rachael Parfitt (ca/frog aw); Jerry Young (br/crocodile). **Getty Images:** Comstock Images (3/ftl/giraffe, ftr, fcl); Photographer's Choice / Burazin (1/ftl/giraffe, 2/ftl/giraffe, cl/giraffe); Stone / Art Wolfe (cla/elephant); Discovery Channel Images / Jeff Foott (1/tr/ants, 2/tr/ants, 3/tr/ants, bl/ants, br/ants); Photodisc / Paul E. Tessier (fcl/bird); Panoramic Images (fcr/bird); Gallo Images / George Brits (fcr/jackal); Stone / Jonathan Knowles (1/cb/porcupine, 2/cb/porcupine); Stockbyte / John Foxx (fbl); Photographer's Choice / Annie Katz (cb/hippo); Photodisc / Steve Allen (crb); Stockbyte / Tom Brakefield (bc/spider, bl/spider, fbr/spider); Gallo Images / Shem Compion (fbr/beetle). **iStockphoto.com:** Christian Musat (1/cra/zebra, c/zebra). **Photolibrary:** Mark Deeble & Victoria Stone (cr/bat eared fox). **Warren Photographic Limited:** (cl/springbok). **73 FLPA:** Gerry Ellis / Minden Pictures (bl, crb/bird). **Getty Images:** Comstock Images (2/fcr/giraffe); Stone / Art Wolfe (bc/elephant); Flickr / Gail Shotlander (ftl, fcl); Image Source (tl, fbr, fcrb); Panoramic Images (1/tc/bird, 2/tc/bird, fcr/bird); Stone / Gravity Giant Productions (cla/baboon, br); Gallo Images / George Brits (ca); Photographer's Choice / Burazin (1/fcr/giraffe); Flickr / Eddie Sin (fbl); Photographer's Choice / Martin Harvey (crb/vulture); Stockbyte / Altrendo Nature (cl/vulture); Martin Harvey / Lifesize (1/cl/lion cub); Digital Vision / Martin Harvey (2/c/lion cub); Wim van den Heever (1/c/wildebeest); Flickr / Paul Lee (2/cr/wildebeest); Photodisc / Theo Allofs (cb/ostrich); Gallo Images / Daryl Balfour (crb/squirrel). **Photolibrary:** Mark Deeble & Victoria Stone (ca/bat eared fox). **Warren Photographic Limited:** (fcla). 7**4 Alamy Images:** Life on white (fbr). **Corbis:** DLILLC (clb). **Dorling Kindersley:** Philip Dowell (fcla); Natural History Museum, London (fcra). **Getty Images:** National Geographic / Gordon Wiltsie (crb); Photographer's Choice / Darrell Gulin (1/tl, 2/tl, 1/tr, 2/tr). **Photolibrary:** Oxford Scientific (OSF) / Ariadne Van Zandbergen (fbl). **75 Alamy Images:** Life on white (ftr); Kevin Schafer (crb). **Corbis:** DLILLC (cra/frog). **Dorling Kindersley:** Philip Dowell (cla, fcrb/leopard); Jerry Young (cl); Natural History Museum, London (fcla, cr); Natural History Museum, London (cra/bug, cr/bug, 1/fcrb, 2/fcrb, 3/fcrb); Rachael Parfitt (fcr/frog aw). **Getty Images:** National Geographic / Gordon Wiltsie (fbr); Photographer's Choice / Darrell Gulin (tc, ca, fcr, cb). **Photolibrary:** Oxford Scientific (OSF) / Ariadne Van Zandbergen (fclb). **76 Corbis:** David Campbell / Visuals Unlimited (ftr); Steve Maslowski / Visuals Unlimited (fcr/shrew). **FLPA:** Jim Brandenburg / Minden Pictures (c); Tom Vezo / Minden Pictures (cra/ground squirrel, cr/ground squirrel). **Getty Images:** National Geographic / Joel Sartore (ca/badger); Photodisc / Life On White (ca/prairie dog, fcra/chipmunk, clb); Riser / Richard Drury (tr, cl); Photographer's Choice / Darrell Gulin (cr/butterfly); Photodisc / Paul E. Tessier (fcr/owl); Stone / Catherine Ledner (bc). **Warren Photographic Limited:** (fcla); Jane Burton (cr/rabbit, br, fbr). **77 Corbis:** David Campbell / Visuals Unlimited (crb). **Dorling Kindersley:** Rachael Parfitt (fcr/frog aw). **FLPA:** Jim Brandenburg / Minden Pictures (tl). **Getty Images:** National Geographic / George Grall (ca, cb); Photodisc / Paul E. Tessier (tc); Stone / Catherine Ledner (fcla); Visuals Unlimited / Joe McDonald (cla, br); Photodisc / Life On White (cl); National Geographic / Joel Sartore (cb); Photographer's Choice / Darrell Gulin (cr/butterfly); Photodisc / Digital Zoo (ftl, cr/skunk). **Warren Photographic Limited:** (bc); Jane Burton (1/tr, 2/tr, 1/cra, 2/cra, fcl). **78 Alamy Images:** Top-Pics TBK (cb/seal); WildLife GmbH (bl/reindeer, cr/reindeer). **Corbis:** Steven Kazlowski / Science Faction (tl/walrus). **FLPA:** Norbert Wu / Minden Pictures (cl/icefish). **Getty Images:** Photographer's Choice / Frank Lukasseck (bc/wolf). **naturepl.com:** Doug Allan (fbl/narwhal); Steven Kazlowski (2/ca/arctic fox, 1/ca/arctic fox, c/seal, ftr, fcl/polar bear, cr/fox); John Cancalosi (tr); Brandon Cole (c/beluga whale); Robin Chittenden (cb/goose, fcra); Elio Della Ferrera (cla/ermine); Wild Wonders of Europe / Zacek (fcla/owl); Doug Perrine (tc/shark, br); Gary K. Smith (fclb/seal, fcrb); Andy Rouse (clb/owl); Juan Carlos Munoz (fcl/wolverine, fbr); Bengt Lundberg (cb/lemming). **79 Alamy Images:** Top-Pics TBK (c/seal). **Corbis:** Steven Kazlowski / Science Faction (cb/walrus). **Dorling Kindersley:** Rachael Parfitt (clb/frog aw). **FLPA:** Norbert Wu / Minden Pictures (c/icefish). **Getty Images:** Photographer's Choice / Frank Lukasseck (fcrb). **naturepl.com:** Doug Allan (ftl/narwhal); Tom Vezo (br); Eric Baccega (fcl); Gabriel Rojo (fcr); Wild Wonders of Europe / Zacek (fclb); Andy Rouse (tc); Bengt Lundberg (crb); Elio Della Ferrera (cla); Steven Kazlowski (fbl, fcra/seal, ca); Brandon Cole (bc). **80 Getty Images:** Digital Vision / Digital Zoo (cl); Panoramic Images (fcr); Workbook Stock / Thomas Kokta (clb); Photographer's Choice / Pam Francis (1/bc/pig, 2/bc/pig, 3/bc/pig); Photographer's Choice / Frank Lukasseck (tc). **Warren Photographic Limited:** (fcra/mallard duckling, 1/cr/rabbit, 2/cr/rabbit, 3/cr/rabbit, 4/cr/rabbit, 5/cr/rabbit, 6/cr/rabbit, cb, 1/crb/cat, 2/crb/cat); Jane Burton (cla); Mark Taylor (fcl). **81 Dorling Kindersley:** Philip Dowell (fcrb/goat); Stephen Oliver (clb/chick); Rachael Parfitt (bc/frog aw). **Getty Images:** Digital Vision / Digital Zoo (cl); Photographer's Choice / Pam Francis (tr/pig, fcl/pig, fbl/pig); Workbook Stock / Thomas Kokta (tc/seal); Photographer's Choice / Frank Lukasseck (cr/penguins); Panoramic Images (crb/lion). **Warren Photographic Limited:** (ftl/duck, tl/rabbit, tr/rabbit, fclb/lamb, ftr/cat, cra/rabbit, fcla/rabbit, fcr/rabbit, fbr/rabbit, bc/cat); Mark Taylor (tc/fawn); Jane Burton (fcr/dog). **82 Dorling Kindersley:** (clb/velociraptor, cr/velociraptor); Royal Tyrrell Museum of Palaeontology, Alberta, Canada (cla/troodon, fcr); Natural History Museum, London - modelmaker (bc/gallimimus); Graham High at Centaur Studios - modelmaker (c/brachiosaurus, bc); Natural History Museum, London (cl/deinonychus, cra/oviraptor); Royal Tyrell Museum (tl/edmontonia); Centaur Studios - modelmakers (tc/triceratops); Jon Hughes (cl/heterodontosaurus); Robert L. Braun - modelmaker (bl/stegosaurus); Rachael Parfitt (br/frog aw). **82-83 Dorling Kindersley:** Robert L. Braun - modelmaker (stegosaurus); Royal Tyrell Museum (edmontonia). **83 Dorling Kindersley:** Centaur Studios - modelmakers (bc); Jon Hughes (c/heterodontosaurus); Graham High at Centaur Studios - modelmaker (cl/brachiosaurus); Natural History Museum, London (fcl); Natural History Museum, London - modelmaker (fcra/gallimimus). **84 Alamy Images:** Arco Images GmbH / I. Schulz (crb). **Dorling Kindersley:** Hunstanton Sea Life Centre, Hunstanton, Norfolk (cl). **naturepl.com:** Shattil & Rozinski (ca). **Warren Photographic Limited:** (cra). **85 Alamy Images:** Arco Images GmbH / I. Schulz (cr, bc). **Dorling Kindersley:** Hunstanton Sea Life Centre, Hunstanton, Norfolk (cl, bl); Rachael Parfitt (cl/frog aw). **naturepl.com:** Shattil & Rozinski (cb, fbl). **Warren Photographic Limited:** (tl, br). **86 FLPA:** Pete Oxford /

Minden Pictures (fbr). **Getty Images:** Photographer's Choice / Darrell Gulin (clb). **iStockphoto.com:** Eric Isselée (fbl); Christian Musat (cla); Skip ODonnell (fcr). **Photolibrary:** Juniors Bildarchiv (tc). **Warren Photographic Limited:** (bc). **87 Dorling Kindersley:** Natural History Museum, London (cla/butterfly, fcra/butterfly, cr/butterfly, cl/butterfly, bc/butterfly, br/butterfly); Rachael Parfitt (ftl/frog aw). **FLPA:** Pete Oxford / Minden Pictures (tl). **Getty Images:** Photographer's Choice / Darrell Gulin (cb). **iStockphoto.com:** Eric Isselée (tr); Christian Musat (bl); Skip ODonnell (bc). **Photolibrary:** Juniors Bildarchiv (cla). **Warren Photographic Limited:** (cl). **88 Alamy Images:** Brand X Pictures (8/crb/bug); Kevin Schafer (8/br/bird). **Corbis:** Hal Beral (9/br/fish); Martin Harvey (2/bl/fish). **Dorling Kindersley:** Booth Museum of Natural History, Brighton (1/cla/butterfly); Natural History Museum, London (3/cla/butterfly); Natural History Museum, London (1/fclb/bug, 2/clb/bug, 5/cb/bug); Jerry Young (4/cb/bug). **Getty Images:** First Light / Doug Hamilton (7/br/bird); Stock Image / Frank Lukasseck (4/bc/bird); National Geographic / Joel Sartore (1/cl/armadillo, 2/cl/armadillo, 3/c/armadillo, 4/c/armadillo). **iStockphoto.com:** Robert Blanchard (5/bc/bird); Paul Tessier (6/bc/bird); Andrew Howe (3/bl/bird, 9/br/bird, 1/bl/bird); Eric Isselée (3/clb/dog, tl/panda). **naturepl.com:** Shattil & Rozinski (2/bl/bird). **Science Photo Library:** Barbara Strnadova (2/cla/butterfly). **Warren Photographic Limited:** (4/cl/rabbit, 7/bc/fish); Mark Taylor (7/crb/dog, 4/cb/dog, 6/cr/cat); Jane Burton (6/cb/dog, 5/cb/dog, 1/fcl/rabbit, 5/c/rabbit, 3/cl/cat, 4/c/cat, 1/fclb/dog, 2/clb/dog). **89 Alamy Images:** Brand X Pictures (fcr/bug); Kevin Schafer (ftr/macaw). **Corbis:** Hal Beral (cla/red fish); Martin Harvey (fcra/striped fish). **Dorling Kindersley:** Booth Museum of Natural History, Brighton (cb/butterfly); Natural History Museum, London (tl/butterfly); Natural History Museum, London (ca/bug, crb/bug, fbl/bug); Jerry Young (fcrb/red bug); Rachael Parfitt (cra/frog aw). **Getty Images:** First Light / Doug Hamilton (fcla/duck); Stock Image / Frank Lukasseck (tc/egret); National Geographic / Joel Sartore (ca/armadillo, cra/armadillo, cb/armadillo, br/armadillo). **iStockphoto.com:** Robert Blanchard (cr/spoonbill); Eric Isselée (c, bc/dog); Paul Tessier (fcr/hummingbird); Andrew Howe (cb/kingfisher, clb/swallow, br/robin). **naturepl.com:** Shattil & Rozinski (tr/jay). **Science Photo Library:** Barbara Strnadova (crb/butterfly). **Warren Photographic Limited:** (tr/goldfish, cra/sandy rabbit); Jane Burton (ftl/bulldog, cra/grey rabbit, cl/shih tzu, clb/boxer, fcrb/cat, fbl/dog, bl/cat, cb/rabbit); Mark Taylor (fcl/grey cat, cl/poodle, br/dog). **90 Alamy Images:** Life on white (ca, fcrb); WildLife GmbH (fcla/reindeer). **Corbis:** Hal Beral (tl/fish, fcr); DLILLC (tc/frog, br). **Dorling Kindersley:** Natural History Museum, London (c). **Warren Photographic Limited:** Jane Burton (clb, ftl/cat). **91 Alamy Images:** WildLife GmbH (tc). **Dorling Kindersley:** Natural History Museum, London (cra). **FLPA:** Michael & Patricia Fogden / Minden Pictures (ca). **Warren Photographic Limited:** Jane Burton (cb, bl). **92 FLPA:** Gerry Ellis / Minden Pictures (bl, bc/bird). **Getty Images:** Photodisc / Theo Allofs (fbr). **93 Corbis:** Frans Lanting (clb). **Dorling Kindersley:** Philip Dowell (fcra). **Getty Images:** Gallo Images / Shem Compion (cb); Workbook Stock / David Maitland (cr). **iStockphoto.com:** Bjorn Heller (br). **naturepl.com:** Steven Kazlowski (crb, fcrb). **94 Getty Images:** Photographer's Choice / Darrell Gulin (tl). **Warren Photographic Limited:** Jane Burton (tr)

Farm chapter

98 Corbis: Ocean (br). **Dorling Kindersley:** Odds Farm Park, High Wycombe, Bucks (tr, ftr). **Dreamstime.com:** Isselee (bl). **Getty Images:** Stone / Bob Elsdale (cr/b, cr/c, fcl/c, fcl/r, c/l, c/c); Taxi / Tony Evans / Timelapse Library (cr/l). **99 Corbis:** Ocean (ftl). **Dorling Kindersley:** Odds Farm Park, High Wycombe, Bucks (cb, crb). **Dreamstime.com:** Isselee (ca/l). **Getty Images:** Digital Vision / ICHIRO (cla/l, c/l); Stone / Catherine Ledner (fcr); Photographer's Choice / Pam Francis (cla/c, c/r). **102 Dorling Kindersley:** Stephen Oliver / Appaloosa - Golden Nugget Sally Chaplin (bl, tr). **Dreamstime.com:** Randy Harris (cla/t); Viktoria Makarova (clb, fbl). **Fotolia:** Eric Isselée (fcla/b, br); Harald Lange (cb, cra). **103 Dorling Kindersley:** Barnabas Kindersley (fbl). **Dreamstime.com:** Randy Harris (tr); Isselee (fcrb); Viktoria Makarova (clb, br). **Fotolia:** Harald Lange (cr). **104 Dorling Kindersley:** South of England Rare Breeds Centre, Ashford, Kent (fclb). **Getty Images:** Image Source (bc); Photodisc / Jules Frazier (fcla). **105 Dorling Kindersley:** Barleylands Farm Museum and Animal Centre, Billericay (cl); South of England Rare Breeds Centre, Ashford, Kent (tc). **Getty Images:** Image Source (cr); Photodisc / Jules Frazier (fcra). **106 Corbis:** Ocean (cl). **Getty Images:** LOOK / Karl Johaentges (clb); Photographer's Choice / Wilfried Krecichwost (cra); Photonica / Amy Eckert (cb); Photographer's Choice / Diane Macdonald (cla); Photolibrary / DogPhoto.Com (cr); Photographer's Choice / Tom Walker (bc). **SuperStock:** Minden Pictures (c). **Warren Photographic Limited:** (ca). **107 Corbis:** Ocean (br). **Getty Images:** LOOK / Karl Johaentges (ca/goats); Photographer's Choice / Mark S. Wexler (bc); Photographer's Choice / Diane Macdonald (tl); Photographer's Choice / Tom Walker (ca/swans); Photolibrary / DogPhoto.Com (cla/puppies); Photographer's Choice / Wilfried Krecichwost (cr); Photonica / Amy Eckert (bl). **SuperStock:** Minden Pictures (clb). **Warren Photographic Limited:** (cl). **108 Alamy Images:** David Wootton (cra). **iStockphoto.com:** Alan Egginton (cla). **New Holland Agriculture:** (fcrb). **109 Alamy Images:** Louis Laliberte (tc, crb); David Wootton (clb). **Alvey and Towers:** (cra). **Dreamstime.com:** Bjorn Heller (cl). **iStockphoto.com:** Alan Egginton (bl). **110 Corbis:** Ken Davies (fcla); Debra Ferguson / AgStock Images (fcl); Gehl Company (cr). **Getty Images:** Cultura / Echo (bc); Gavin Hellier / Robert Harding (crb); Flickr / Boston Thek Imagery (fbl); National Geographic / Pete Mcbride (cl). **111 Alvey and Towers:** (bl). **Corbis:** Ken Davies (cb); Debra Ferguson / AgStock Images (ftl); Gehl Company (fcla). **Getty Images:** Cultura / Echo (ftl); Digital Vision / Alistair Berg (fcra); Flickr / Boston Thek Imagery (ca); Gavin Hellier / Robert Harding (fcr); National Geographic / Pete Mcbride (bc). **112 Alamy Images:** (c/courgettes); blickwinkel / McPHOTO / KPA (cla); foodfolio (cl/blueberries); Keith Leighton (fbl). **113 Alamy Images:** (tc); blickwinkel / McPHOTO / KPA (c/tangerines); Bon Appetit / Buntrock, Gerrit Ltd. (tl/potatoes, fbr); Pixmann (fbl). **Getty Images:** Foodcollection RF (cl/grapes). **114 Warren Photographic Limited:** (ftl/b). **115 Dreamstime.com:** Bjorn Heller (cra). **Getty Images:** Photographer's Choice / Pam Francis (cr/cow); Stone / Bob Elsdale (tl, cla/l, cla/r). **Warren Photographic Limited:** (bl/ducklings, bl/mouse). **116 Dorling Kindersley:** South of England Rare Breeds Centre, Ashford, Kent (fcra). **Dreamstime.com:** Isselee (cl, fclb); Claudia Steininger (fbr). **Getty Images:** Flonline / Beate Zoellner (crb); Stone / Joe Toreno (fbl); National Geographic / Joel Sartore (cla). **Warren Photographic Limited:** (fcl, fcla, fcrb). **117 Dorling Kindersley:** South of England Rare Breeds Centre, Ashford, Kent (c). **Dreamstime.com:** Isselee (ftl, cl/kitten); Claudia Steininger (fcra). **Getty Images:** Flonline / Beate Zoellner (tr); National Geographic / Joel Sartore (ca); Stone / Joe Toreno (crb/donkey). **Warren Photographic Limited:** (clb/dog, cb/goat, fbr). **118 Corbis:** Pat Doyle (tl/ginger kittens). **Dorling Kindersley:** Museo Gauchesco Ricardo Guiraldes (ca); Jamie Marshall (c); Queen's Rangers (fcr/hatchet). **119 Corbis:** Pat Doyle (crb/kittens). **Dorling Kindersley:** Museo Gauchesco Ricardo Guiraldes (tl); Queen's Rangers (ftr); Jamie Marshall (cra/shovel). **120 Corbis:** Pat Doyle (fcrb). **Dreamstime.com:** Isselee (fclb, crb). **Fotolia:** Eric Isselée (cl/dog). **Getty Images:** Stone / Bob Elsdale (fcla). **121 Warren Photographic Limited:** (tc). **122 Dorling Kindersley:** Tablehurst Farm (fcrb). **Getty Images:** Nicholas Eveleigh (ftr/l); Photographer's Choice / Sam Armstrong (ftr/r); Sudres Jean-Daniel / Hemis.fr (ftl); FoodPix / Paula Hible (cb/l). **123 Dorling Kindersley:** Tablehurst Farm (ftr/sausages). **Getty Images:** Nicholas Eveleigh (fbr/l); Photographer's Choice / Sam Armstrong (fbr/r); FoodPix / Paula Hible (br). **124 Dorling Kindersley:** Jamie Marshall (cra). **Getty Images:** AFP Photo / Francois Nascimbeni (fcrb); Robert Harding World Imagery / Annie Owen (crb); StockImage / Frederic Pacorel (fcla); Aurora / Aaron Ansarov (clb); Marc Serota (ftr); Stone / Denis Waugh (tl); Stone+ / Nicolas Russell (fcra); First Light / Benjamin Rondel (cla); Oxford Scientific / Mike Hill (ftl); National Geographic / Joel Sartore (fbr); Gerard Sioen / Gamma-Rapho (fcla). **125 Dorling Kindersley:** Jamie Marshall (fcl); Rough Guides (ftl). **Getty Images:** AFP Photo / Pierre Andrieu (tr/horses); National Geographic / Joel Sartore (tl); Gerard Sioen / Gamma-Rapho (tr); Marc Serota (fcla); Oxford Scientific / Mike Hill (cra); StockImage / Frederic Pacorel (fcra); Stone / Denis Waugh (cr); Stone+ / Nicolas Russell (c); Robert Harding World Imagery / Annie Owen (crb); Aurora / Aaron Ansarov (fcrb); AFP Photo / Francois Nascimbeni (fbl); First Light / Benjamin Rondel (br). **126 Corbis:** DLILLC (cla/flower / l, cla/flower / r). **Dorling Kindersley:** Stephen Oliver / Appaloosa - Golden Nugget Sally Chaplin (tl). **Getty Images:** Photodisc / GK Hart / Vikki Hart (bl/cow / l, bl/cow / r, bc/cow / l, bc/cow / c, bc/cow / r, br/cow / l, br/cow / r, fbr/cow / l, fbr/cow / r); Photographer's Choice / Pam Francis (cla/pig / l, cla/pig / r, ca); Taxi / Tony Evans / Timelapse Library (cl/lamb / l, cl/lamb / r, c/lamb / l, c/lamb / r). **Warren Photographic Limited:** (clb/goat / l, clb/goat / r, cb/goat / l, cb/goat / c, cb/goat / r, crb/goat / l, crb/goat / r). **127 Corbis:** DLILLC (tc/flower, crb/flower). **Dorling Kindersley:** Stephen Oliver / Appaloosa - Golden Nugget Sally Chaplin (fbr/horse). **Fotolia:** Tan Kian Khoon (ftl/butterfly, tl/butterfly, fcra/butterfly / t, fcra/butterfly / b, cra/butterfly / l, cra/butterfly / r, ca/butterfly / l, ca/butterfly / r, cl/butterfly, c/butterfly / l, c/butterfly / r, fcrb/butterfly, clb/butterfly, cb/butterfly / t, cb/butterfly / b, fcl/butterfly, fclb/butterfly / t, fclb/butterfly / b, fbl/butterfly, bl/butterfly). **Getty Images:** Photodisc / GK Hart / Vikki Hart (tl/cow, ftr/cow, ca/cow, cra/cow, cl/cow, fcr/cow, fcrb/cow, cb/cow, clb/cow); Photographer's Choice / Pam Francis (tl/pig, ftl/pig, fbl/pig); Taxi / Tony Evans / Timelapse Library (tc/lamb, fcr/lamb, fclb/lamb, fcrb/lamb). **Warren Photographic Limited:** (fcla/goat, cla/goat, tr/goat, cra/goat, c/goat, fclb/goat, bc/goat). **128 Corbis:** Digital Zoo (cla, bc); Ocean (c). **Dreamstime.com:** Bjorn Heller (cla, clb). **Fotolia:** Anatolii (ftr, cl). **Getty Images:** AFP Photo / Francois Nascimbeni (crb). **Warren Photographic Limited:** (fcla). **129 Dorling Kindersley:** Lindsey Stock (cla, cb). **Warren Photographic Limited:** (cr). **130 Corbis:** Ocean (cra). **131 Dorling Kindersley:** Stephen Oliver (ftl). **Warren Photographic Limited:** (cra/stretching). **132 Corbis:** Ocean (tl). **133 Dorling Kindersley:** Stephen Oliver / Appaloosa - Golden Nugget Sally Chaplin (cr). **134 Dorling Kindersley:** Barnabas Kindersley (cra). **135 Dorling Kindersley:** Barnabas Kindersley (fclb). **136 Alamy Images:** Bon Appetit / Buntrock, Gerrit Ltd. (fcrb). **Dorling Kindersley:** Alan Buckingham (fbr). **Dreamstime.com:** Svetlana Mihailova (fclb). **Getty Images:** DAJ (fcra). **New Holland Agriculture:** (tl). **137 Alamy Images:** (cb); Bon Appetit / Buntrock, Gerrit Ltd. (fcr). **Dorling Kindersley:** Alan Buckingham (fbr). **Dreamstime.com:** Svetlana Mihailova (fcla). **Getty Images:** DAJ (ftr). **New Holland Agriculture:** (c). **138 Alamy Images:** Pixmann (cr). **Dorling Kindersley:** Barleylands Farm Museum and Animal Centre, Billericay (fcr). **Getty Images:** Digital Vision / Alistair Berg (fclb). **141 Alamy Images:** foodfolio (fbl). **Alvey and Towers:** (tr). **Dorling Kindersley:** Rough Guides (fcr)

Things That Go chapter

144 Dorling Kindersley: Dmitry Kalinovsky / Shutterstock (ca/van); wacpan / Shutterstock (ftl/bicycle); Maksim Toome / Shutterstock (tl); Olaru Radian-Alexandru / Shutterstock (tc, fcra); Petr Student / Shutterstock (clb/coach); Rob Wilson / Shutterstock (crb/white pick up truck); National Railway Museum, York (ftl/bicycle with basket, crb/bicycle); Regien Paassen / Shutterstock (fcl/school bus, cra). **145 Dorling Kindersley:** Dmitry Kalinovsky / Shutterstock (c); Petr Student / Shutterstock (fbr/coach); Maksim Toome / Shutterstock (cl); wacpan / Shutterstock (fcr/bicycle). **146 Dorling Kindersley:** Edgar Gillingwater - modelmaker (tr, cb); The Shuttleworth Collection, Bedfordshire (cla, c/triplane); Paul Wilkinson (cr/helicopter). **147 Dorling Kindersley:** Paul Wilkinson (cla/burgundy helicopter). 148 **Dorling Kindersley:** Gary Blakeley / Shutterstock (fcra); R. Peterkin / Shutterstock (ftr, ca); Search and Rescue Hovercraft, Richmond, British Columbia (cl). **149 Dorling Kindersley:** Anyka / Shutterstock (tl, cl/container ship); Search and Rescue Hovercraft, Richmond, British Columbia (ftl); Gary Blakeley / Shutterstock (c/speedboat). **150 Dorling Kindersley:** Demetrio Carrasco / Rough Guides (cla, tr); Chris Christoforou / Rough Guides (cl); The Science Museum, London (clb); Tim Draper / Rough Guides (cb, ftr); Museum of Transportation, St Louis, Missouri (fbl); National Railway Museum, York (bc, cr, crb); Eddie Gerald / Rough Guides (fcl). **151 Dorling Kindersley:** Chris Christoforou / Rough Guides (cb); tonyz20 / Shutterstock (cla); Museum of Transportation, St Louis, Missouri (tl); Eddie Gerald / Rough Guides (cr); The Science Museum, London (fbr). **152 Dorling Kindersley:** Faraways / Shutterstock (cla). **Scania CV AB (publ):** (cl). **153 Dorling Kindersley:** Faraways / Shutterstock (bl). **Scania CV AB (publ):** (tc). **154 Dorling Kindersley:** greenland / Shutterstock (ftl). **PunchStock:** Steve Smith (tr). **155 Dorling Kindersley:** greenland / Shutterstock (cla). **PunchStock:** Steve Smith (tr). **156 Dorling Kindersley:** Conrad GMBH - modelmaker (fcl, cl). **156-157 Dorling Kindersley:** Balfour Beatty Major Projects (road building) (t). **157 Dorling Kindersley:** Conrad GMBH - modelmaker (c, cr). **158 Dorling Kindersley:** Aberdeen Fire Department, Maryland (ftl); Andreas Altenburger / Shutterstock (fcla); Halima Ahkdar / Shutterstock (c/police car, br); Bergen County, NJ, Law and Public Safety Institute (ca, cra); Volunteer Medical Service Corps, Lansdale, Pennsylvania (clb); Cockermouth Mountain Rescue Team, England (bl); Fire crew at Logan International Airport, Boston, Massachusetts (bc); RNLI - Royal National Lifeboat Institution, and crew (fcl/inflatable lifeboat, ftr). **159 Dorling Kindersley:** Aberdeen Fire Department, Maryland (bc); Cockermouth Mountain Rescue Team, England (cl); Andreas Altenburger / Shutterstock (cb); Volunteer Medical Service Corps, Lansdale, Pennsylvania (cr); Fire crew at Logan International Airport, Boston, Massachusetts (br). **160 Case IH Agriculture:** (bl, crb). **Dorling Kindersley:** Miller Mining (c). **New Holland Agriculture:** (tc, cra, br). **161 Case IH Agriculture:** (tr/sprayer, bl). **Dorling Kindersley:** Miller Mining (ca/muck spreader). **New Holland Agriculture:** (ftl/baler, tr/tractor, ftr/seed drill, cl/baler, fclb). **162 Dorling Kindersley:** Goodwood Festival of Speed (cl/porsche, cr); National Motor Museum, Beaulieu (tl). **163 Dorling Kindersley:** National Motor Museum, Beaulieu (cla); Nikid Design Ltd (clb). **164 Dorling Kindersley:** Tim Draper / Rough Guides (cl/moon, crb); The Science Museum, London (tl, tc, cra, cb, ftr); Eurospace Center, Transinne, Belgium (fcla); NASA (fclb, fbl, br). **165 Dorling Kindersley:** Eurospace Center, Transinne, Belgium (tc); Bob Gathany (tl); NASA (cb). **166 Dorling Kindersley:** NASA (clb); R. Peterkin / Shutterstock (tr). **PunchStock:** Brand X Pictures (cb). **167 Dorling Kindersley:** NASA (bl); R. Peterkin / Shutterstock (clb). **PunchStock:** Brand X Pictures (c). **168 Dorling Kindersley:** Brookes and Vernons / JCB (ftr); Ted Taylor - modelmaker (clb, crb); National Motor Museum, Beaulieu (bl). **169 Dorling Kindersley:** Brookes and Vernons / JCB (clb); Ted Taylor - modelmaker (fcrb/t, fcrb/b, br). **New Holland Agriculture:** (cla, fbr). **170 Dorling Kindersley:** Aberdeen Fire Department, Maryland (tl); Dmitry Kalinovsky / Shutterstock (clb). **171 Dorling Kindersley:** Adisa / Shutterstock (cla); Regien Paassen / Shutterstock (clb). **New Holland Agriculture:** (bl). **Scania CV AB (publ):** (tl). **172 (c) Ford Motor Company Limited:** (ka 1, ka 2, ka 3, ka 4, ka 5, ka 6, ka 7, ka 8, ka 9). **173 (c) Ford Motor Company Limited:** (tl/ka, tr/ka, fcla/ka, ca/ka, c/ka, cl/ka, fcrb/ka, bl/ka, br/ka). **175 Dorling Kindersley:** Armé Museum, Stockholm, Sweden (fcla/cannon, br). **176 Dorling Kindersley:** Cockermouth Mountain Rescue Team, England (fcl); RAF Wittering, Cambridgeshire (fcra). **177 Dorling Kindersley:** Ian Aitken / Rough Guides (ftl, ftr); The Science Museum, London (tl). **180 Dorling Kindersley:** Sean Hunter (fcra/arrow). **182 Dorling Kindersley:** Andreas Altenburger / Shutterstock (fclb); Ted Taylor - modelmaker (ftl/t, ftl/c, ftl/b); American 50's Car Hire (cra); London Transport Museum (c/t, c/ca, c/cb, c/b); Petr Student / Shutterstock (fcr). **New Holland Agriculture:** (ftr). **PunchStock:** Image Source (cb). **183 Dorling Kindersley:** Andreas Altenburger / Shutterstock (ftl); American 50's Car Hire (cla); Ted Taylor - modelmaker (tl/t, tl/c, tl/b); Petr Student / Shutterstock (ftr); London Transport Museum (cb/t, cb/ca, cb/cb, cb/b). **New Holland Agriculture:** (ca). **PunchStock:** Image Source (fcla). **186 Dorling Kindersley:** Balfour Beatty Major Projects (road building); National Railway Museum, York (fcl); Rob Wilson / Shutterstock (fcr); Bob Gathany (fclb). **New Holland Agriculture:** (fcla)

All other images © Dorling Kindersley
For further information see: www.dkimages.com